THE KYOTO MECHANISMS AND RUSSIAN CLIMATE POLITICS

Arild Moe and
Kristian Tangen

THE ROYAL INSTITUTE OF
INTERNATIONAL AFFAIRS
Energy and Environment Programme

© Royal Institute of International Affairs, 2000

Published in Great Britain in 2000
by the Royal Institute of International Affairs,
Chatham House, 10 St James's Square, London SW1Y 4LE
(Charity Registration No. 208 223)

Distributed worldwide by the Brookings Institution,
1775 Massachusetts Avenue, NW, Washington, DC 20036-2188

All rights reserved. No part of this publication may be reproduced,
stored in a retrieval system, or transmitted by any other means without
the prior written permission of the copyright holder. Please direct all
inquiries to the publishers.

ISBN 1 86203 125 8

Cover design by Matthew Link
Printed and bound in Great Britain by the Chameleon Press Ltd

*The Royal Institute of International Affairs is an independent body which
promotes the rigorous study of international questions and does not express
opinions of its own. The opinions expressed in this publication are the
responsibility of the author.*

HC
340.12
.Z9
A4
2000

CONTENTS

	List of figures and tables	v
	Abbreviations	vi
	Acknowledgments	viii
1	Introduction	1
2	Russia in the international climate negotiations	7
	Introduction	7
	Russia as the third-largest emitter	8
	Economic interests based on the energy situation	10
	Russia's international positioning: from OPEC to JUSSCANNZ	12
	Policies and measures	18
	How stable is Russian policy?	23
3	Trends in energy consumption and emissions	28
	Russian economic and energy trends	28
	Emission trends	34
	Alternative scenarios	37
4	The emerging climate regime – challenges and opportunities for Russia	44
	What will be Russia's piece of the quota market pie?	44
	Russia's power in the quota market	46

	International restrictions on emissions trading	48
	Conclusion	52
5	Domestic Russian implementation	54
	What is at stake?	55
	Who are the actors?	57
	The debate over surplus quotas	65
	'Implementation games'	71
6	Gazprom – A key actor	79
	Gazprom in the Russian economy	79
	Gazprom's greenhouse gas emissions	81
	Is the industry structure sustainable?	86
	Export strategy	90
	Ready for implementation?	94
7	Gas exports, emissions trading and JI – Four scenarios	96
	Scenario 1: quota sales as a source of income	97
	Scenario 2: joint implementation and industrial cooperation	99
	Scenario 3: quota sales and gas exports	101
	Scenario 4: climate change as a threat to Gazprom's operations	104
8	Conclusions	107

LIST OF FIGURES AND TABLES

Figures

3.1	Macroeconomic indicators and fuel consumption 1990–9	29
3.2	Energy consumption, 1990–9	33
3.3	Implicit forecast of fuel consumption, 2010	36
3.4	GDP growth (%), 1990–9	38
4.1	Price formation under monopoly	47

Tables

2.1	Greenhouse gas emissions in the Russian Federation, 1990 and 1994	9
3.1	Total emissions, 1990 and 1994, and official emission scenarios, 2000–2010	37
3.2	Restructuring and growth: assumptions and output	40
3.3	Stagnation: assumptions and output	41
3.4	Sustained decline: assumptions and output	41
6.1	Greenhouse gas emissions from gas industry operations, 1998	84
6.2	Direct greenhouse gas emissions: Gazprom compared to other emitters	85

ABBREVIATIONS

AIJ	activities implemented jointly
BCM	billion cubic metres
CDM	clean development mechanism
CMEA	Council for Mutual Economic Assistance
COP	Conference of the Parties
EBRD	European Bank for Reconstruction and Development
ET	emissions trading
ERU	emission reduction units
FNI	Fridtjof Nansen Institute
GDP	Gross Domestic Product
GHG	greenhouse gas
GNP	Gross National Product
ICC	Interagency Commission of the Russian Federation on Climate Change Problems
IEA	International Energy Agency
IMEMO	Institute of World Economy and International Relations
INC	International Negotiation Committee
IPCC	International Panel on Climate Change
JI	joint implementation
JUSSCANNZ	Japan/United States/Switzerland/Canada/Australia/Norway/New Zealand
Mt	million tonnes
MtC	million tonnes of carbon
NGO	non-governmental organization

OECD	Organization for Economic Cooperation and Development
OPEC	Oil Producing and Exporting Countries
UNFCCC	United Nations Framework Convention on Climate Change

ACKNOWLEDGMENTS

The Petropol programme of the Norwegian Research Council has financed the research behind this report (Project No. 127108/510). The authors are grateful to the programme board for the initial idea of coupling the Fridtjof Nansen Institute's long-term focus on the Russian gas industry with its research on the development of an international climate regime. A reference group composed of Solveig Glomsrød, Ole Gunnar Austvik and Lars Erik Aamot gave valuable input in the middle of the project. Gesine Hasselmeier of the FNI did a thorough job in searching for literature and then co-authoring a discussion paper that formed the basis for Chapter 2. Elena Nikitina of IMEMO gave insightful comments to the same discussion paper and Christiaan Vrolijk of the Royal Institute of International Affairs commented on a draft for Chapter 3. Steinar Andresen of the FNI has been an important discussion partner all the way. Very valuable input was received from a study group organized by the Royal Institute of International Affairs, which commented upon the first version of the report. Nevertheless, none of those mentioned above bear any responsibility for the content or conclusions of the final report.

A.M. and K.T.

1 INTRODUCTION

The climate issue came to the forefront in the scientific community in the second half of the 1980s, and from 1991 it was prominent on the international political agenda. The United Nations Framework Convention on Climate Change (UNFCCC) and the ensuing Kyoto Protocol (1997) represent a unique attempt at regulating human activity by way of international agreements. The potential repercussions of a binding climate treaty on economic development throughout the world are considerable, but exactly how and when the effects will become manifest is unclear, as agreement has not been reached concerning implementation of the convention.

The use of energy, in both volume and form, is at the centre of attention because greenhouse gas (GHG) emissions are closely linked to fossil fuel consumption. The manner in which the world consumes energy will naturally affect not only consumers but also the producers and exporters of energy. Thus countries with high levels of energy exports have had a special stake in the outcome of the international climate negotiations from the very beginning.

To alleviate the adverse economic effects of comprehensive limits on greenhouse gas emissions, flexibility mechanisms, also referred to as the Kyoto mechanisms, were included in the Kyoto Protocol. The purpose of these mechanisms is to ensure that measures designed to curb emissions would be cost-effective by channelling investments in energy efficiency and energy conservation to countries and projects where the cost per unit of emissions reduction is lowest. This concept would entail a large-scale resource transfer from relatively energy-efficient, high-cost countries to energy-inefficient, low-cost countries.

The establishment of emissions reduction targets was a very complicated issue in the early phase of the international negotiations. Many countries could point to special circumstances that justified a more lenient treatment of them compared to other countries. This argument was accepted to a limited extent. Notably, Russia and Ukraine were given a zero target, in contrast to most other industrialized countries, which would have to reduce their emissions by 2010.

Several Annex I countries were given targets that are likely to be above what their emissions would be even if no measures are taken to reduce them. For example, both Germany and the UK may well have 'unused assigned amounts' when the internal EU reallocation is discounted. Also, excess quotas are likely for many of the countries in transition, such as Bulgaria, Romania and Poland. However, most attention has been given to the excess quotas of Russia and also Ukraine. The 'unused assigned amounts', often rather derogatorily named 'hot air', of these countries became a bone of contention in discussions about the implementation of the protocol and the flexibility mechanisms. The sheer size of the Russian and Ukrainian 'unused assigned amounts' is the main reason for this. As we shall discuss later in this report, the 'unused assigned amounts' of Russia alone could meet as much as 50 per cent of the total demand for quotas, making Russia one of the Great Powers in the emissions trading market.

In the West the 'hot air' is often regarded as an easily fulfillable commitment, constituting something of an administrative option, with real cuts as a fallback. The Russian perspective is rather different, however. Back in 1990, the prevalent expectation was that energy consumption and emissions would continue to rise. The drop in emissions was caused by a cataclysmic event – the breakdown of the old political and economic system – and certainly has not been cost-free. Thus Russia's surplus quotas are very different from, for example, Britain's 'hot air', which has come about as a result of restructuring and economic growth. Income from the sale of Russia's surplus quotas is regarded not as a windfall but as compensation for the serious problems that country has endured.

But even without the 'hot air' the scope for emissions trading is very large. The Soviet economic system was extremely energy-intensive, partly because of the abundance of energy resources, and the potential for improvement has not yet been tapped. In fact, the drop in energy consumption since 1990 has been less than the fall in economic activity. In other words, the energy intensity of the Russian economy has increased. This puts the country squarely in the position of a potentially very large recipient of GHG-mitigating investments.

At the same time, the energy industries are a very important part of the Russian economy. Russia is self-sufficient in energy and is also one of the world's largest energy exporters. It is either the third- or fourth-largest crude oil exporter in the world (the second-largest oil exporter if oil products are included) and by far the world's largest natural gas exporter. It is obvious that the climate regime will fundamentally affect Russia's economic interests. Exporting hydrocarbons is the backbone of its economy, and any contraction in foreign markets for them would be a serious threat. This situation leads us to expect that Russia's energy sector interests will engage themselves strongly in the country's positioning during the climate negotiations and also participate actively in the development of a scheme for the domestic implementation of the Kyoto Protocol.

This report seeks to identify the development of a Russian climate policy, with special consideration of the link with energy sector developments. It seeks explanations in empirical evidence for the positions taken and also analyses possible further developments based on evaluations of the emerging climate regime. It examines the changing power configuration among various national public and private actors in relation to climate politics. To some extent our investigation is assisted by considering evidence from studies of climate politics in other countries, but sensitivity to the rapidly changing political and economic landscape in Russia is clearly required too.

Although all hydrocarbon energy fuels and their non-carbon substitutes will be affected by a comprehensive climate regime, natural gas occupies a special position among hydrocarbon fuels because it is more 'greenhouse-friendly' per unit of consumed energy than oil and coal. There also happens to be an abundance of natural gas in Russia, an abundance which hitherto has accorded it a dominant position among domestic fuel supplies, as a result of which it now accounts for more than 50 per cent of primary energy consumption, a unique position among countries with natural gas resources. It has also made Russia the main external supplier to the European gas market and given it a crucial role in the further development of European energy supplies. The question is, how do these perspectives relate to the climate regime? Will climate politics hamper Russian gas exports or, on the contrary, will they offer new opportunities for Russian gas in the export markets? This report discusses possible developments.

In Chapter 2, we address the Russian position in the international climate negotiations. As Russia is important both as an exporter and as a consumer of fossil energy, it would seem at first sight that the energy sector's interests would be reflected in the positions it has taken. This chapter discusses the extent to which this has happened and how that sector's interests have influenced the Russian positions.

Chapter 3 reviews trends in Russia's economy and energy consumption and discusses the potential for Russian surplus quotas. Chapter 4 asks how much of the Kyoto obligations could be met by such quotas and how trade will be organized. We point to the fact that Russia could have considerable power in a future quota market. This potential power, along with the more detailed provisions for emissions trading (ET) and joint implementation (JI), will have important consequences for Russia's domestic fulfilment of the Kyoto Protocol.

The power struggle over Russia's future climate policy and the domestic implementation of the Kyoto mechanisms is still in an early phase. Most of the potential actors seem only faintly aware of the possible gains for those who take part in emissions trading and joint implementation. In Chapter 5 we discuss who the potential actors are, their interests and their institutional powers. The constellation of interests sketched there indicates the set-up for the future power struggle over Russia's climate policy.

Chapter 6 considers why the Russian gas company Gazprom is likely to be an important player in this struggle. Institutionally Gazprom is well suited to handle quota trading. It has relevant experience and controls a large number of low-cost abatement options. Although the climate regime represents a considerable financial risk for most large emitters, Gazprom, we argue, stands a very good chance of gaining from the implementation of a climate policy.

The extent to which Gazprom loses or gains from this implementation could have important consequences for its market strategies. In Chapter 7 we develop four scenarios to illustrate this. In the first three, Gazprom controls a large share of the Russian quotas and, in all except the fourth, it gains from the implementation of a Russian climate policy. There is considerable convergence among three of the four scenarios concerning the effects on gas prices and the competitive position of Russian gas in the European market. Chapter 8 sums up our previous findings.

2 RUSSIA IN THE INTERNATIONAL CLIMATE NEGOTIATIONS

Introduction

Russia has become a potentially important player in the emerging international climate regime. This is a relatively new development. As recently as 1992 there was little mention of Russia as an active participant. The reason for this development is the introduction of flexibility mechanisms as a means of distributing the burden of compliance with the climate convention in a cost-effective manner. The academic and policy debate had gone on for some time,[1] but when the mechanisms were incorporated in the Kyoto Protocol as of the third Conference of the Parties to the Climate Convention – COP 3 – in 1997, they were not spelled out beyond the statement that emissions trading, joint implementation and the clean development mechanism (CDM) would be developed and permitted. The elaboration of the mechanisms is of continuing concern and is scheduled to be resolved at COP 6 by the end of the year 2000. However, the main elements are clear. Two of the mechanisms are relevant for Russia: international emissions trading, whereby one country can sell emission quotas to another country, and joint implementation, whereby

---

[1] See Michael Grubb with Christiaan Vrolijk and Duncan Brack, *The Kyoto Protocol: A Guide and Assessment* (London: RIIA/Earthscan, 1999), pp. 87–96.

two countries undertake a joint emission-reducing project in the country where such a project is more cost-effective. The implementation of these two mechanisms can make Russia a major supplier of emission quotas to other Annex I countries.

This chapter surveys Russia's participation in the climate regime negotiations, relates it to the country's energy situation and also seeks explanations for the positions it has taken at the political level. The overriding questions are: what is the driving force behind the development of Russia's climate policy positions, and are these positions stable?

Russia as the third-largest emitter

The emissions from energy production and consumption in the Russian Federation in 1990 amounted to about 2,400 million tonnes (Mt) CO_2 equivalent, accounting for about 11 per cent of global CO_2 emissions and tying Russia with China for second place after the US in the table of world emitters. These and emissions for other relevant greenhouse gases are presented in Table 2.1. Between 1990 and 1994 CO_2 emissions were reduced by 30 per cent, CH_4 emissions by 26 per cent and N_2O emissions by 43 per cent.

The energy sector and the combustion of fossil fuels are the dominant sources of CO_2 emissions, accounting for 98 per cent of total emissions. Industrial processes, in particular cement production, account for the remainder. Among the fossil fuels 45 per cent of CO_2 emissions are related to natural gas, 30.6 per cent to coal

Table 2.1: Greenhouse gas emissions in the Russian Federation, 1990 and 1994

Greenhouse gas	1990 (Mt)	1900 (Mt CO$_2$ equiv.)	Global share (%) 1990	1994 (Mt)	1994 (Mt CO$_2$ equiv.)
CO$_2$ (carbon dioxide)	647.3[a]	2372	11.0	452.6[a]	1660
CH$_4$ (methane)	26.5	557	7.2	19.61	412
N$_2$O (nitrous oxide)	0.2257	70	10.0	0.1276	40
Others[b] (PFC, SF$_4$, S$_2$F$_6$, HFC-23, HFC-134a)	n/a	40	n/a	n/a	40
Total		3039			2152

[a] MtC = million tonnes of carbon.

[b] Estimate.

Source: The data are compiled from *Vtoroye natsionalnoye soobschenie Rossiyskoy Federatsii* (Second National Communication of the Russian Federation) (1998), Interagency Commission of the Russian Federation on Climate Change Problems, Moscow. As of autumn 2000 this was available only in the Russian language. It is interesting to note that the data compilation presented in the Interagency Commission's First National Communication of the Russian Federation (1995) did not quite meet the methodological standards of the International Panel on Climate Change. This was elaborated in the in-depth review, in which the lack of transparency and compatibility of the emission inventory was criticized (see UNFCCC (1997), 'Report on the In-depth Review of the National Communication of the Russian Federation' at *http://www.unfccc.int/resource/docs/idr/rus01.htm*, sec. 51). With regard to aggregate emission data there are, however, only small differences in the data on CO$_2$ and CH$_4$ emissions reported for 1990 between the First and Second National Communications. The figure for N$_2$O emissions is, however, substantially smaller in the Second National Communication: 225,000 tonnes compared to 820,000 tonnes in the First National Communication. Furthermore, the Second National Communication includes estimates of 'other gases', which the first did not.

and 24.4 per cent to oil. The energy sector was the dominant source of CH_4 emissions – 68 per cent in 1994. Agriculture accounted for 20 per cent; the burning of waste caused 10 per cent, and 2 per cent came from forest fires. The main source of N_2O emissions was agriculture (88 per cent).[2]

Russia is large in terms of emissions, and its CO_2 sink capacity in forests is very high compared to other Annex I countries. According to the review team for the First National Communication (1995), this capacity corresponds to up to 25 per cent of the country's total CO_2 emissions.[3] In the Second National Communication (1998) the estimate is even higher – 34 per cent.[4]

Economic interests based on the energy situation

Russia possesses the largest fossil fuel reservoir in the world. Furthermore, it is one of the world's largest producers, as well as a major consumer and exporter of organic fuels (oil, gas, coal and peat). Russia is the leading producer and largest exporter of natural gas and is the third-largest oil-producer; it is also among the four largest oil-exporters.[5] Natural gas is the dominant fuel in the domestic economy, accounting for about 51 per cent of primary energy consumption. Gas accounts for 42 per cent of electricity production.

The energy complex accounts for about 30 per cent of industrial output in Russia. During recent years it

[2] *Vtoroye natsionalnoye soobschenie.*
[3] UNFCCC, 'Report on the In-depth Review', sec. 7.
[4] *Vtoroye natsionalnoye soobschenie.*
[5] BP Amoco, *Statistical Review of World Energy*, 1999.

accounted for some 55-60 per cent of the income in the federal budget, as well as for 45-50 per cent of the country's export revenues.[6]

The energy sector enjoyed a very high priority in the centrally planned economy. Owing to the low price put on capital and the Soviet economy's almost insatiable demand for energy in combination with abundant reserves, the sector grew to enormous proportions. After the dissolution of the USSR and the abolition of the centrally planned economy, the sector, now organized as joint stock companies with private, public or mixed ownership, has experienced many difficulties associated with a production structure that has become very costly in the new economic framework. Nevertheless, the major oil companies and the gas company Gazprom are in a better position than most other industries; and they form cornerstones in the financial-industrial groups that have become extremely important in the Russian economy.[7] The sector is commonly regarded as crucial in further economic development in Russia: 'The fuel and energy sphere is in the conditions of Russia a most important factor in securing the functioning of society and its social and economic well-being.'[8] One would expect the companies in this sector to be very sensitive to any development that could limit their operations or export potential and also expect that their arguments would have sway with the authorities.

[6] *TEK Rossii: Vchera, Segodnya, Zavtra* ... (Moscow: Institute of Energy Strategy, 1998).
[7] Valery Kryukov and Arild Moe, 'Banks and the Financial Sector', in David Lane (ed.), *The Political Economy of Russian Oil* (Oxford: Rowman & Littlefield, 1999).
[8] *TEK Rossii*.

Russia's international positioning: from OPEC to JUSSCANNZ

Pre-Kyoto positions

The persistent position of the Soviet Union concerning international agreements on specific targets to reduce GHG emissions was that more scientific research was needed on the impact of global climate change before specific reduction targets could be determined.[9] Many Soviet scientists also argued that climate change would have positive consequences for the country, improving the conditions for agriculture etc.[10] Such viewpoints are still supported by some Russian scientists.[11]

The Russian Federation took over the USSR's seat in the climate negotiations while other former Soviet republics now attend under their own state flag. In general, Russia has played a rather reserved role in the international climate negotiations. But the official Russian position concedes the negative effects of climate change, such as the retreat of the permafrost zone and the creation of huge dry areas, resulting in serious economic and agricultural problems. Kotov and Nikitina considered this view as one reason why the Russian Federation

---

[9] OECD/ IEA, *Climate Change Policy Initiatives* (Paris: OECD/IEA, 1992), p. 146; Philip Pryde (1991), *Environmental Management in the Soviet Union* (Cambridge: Cambridge University Press, 1991), p. 31.
[10] See, for example, Kåre Dahl Martinsen, *Sovjetunionen og klimaendringene*, Report 13/1990 (Lysaker: Fridtjof Nansen Institute, 1990).
[11] For a recent example, see V. V. Klimenko, 'Energeticheskie i klimaticheskie aspekty razvitiya Rossii v XXI stoletii', *Gazovaya Promyshlennost*, no. 12, 1997, pp. 21–5.

signed the UNFCCC in 1992.[12] Russia belongs to the industrialized countries listed in Annex I to the UNFCCC and to the countries in transition under this category.

Russia's behaviour at COP 1 (the first Conference of the Parties to the UNFCCC) in Berlin in 1995 has been described as 'defensive and almost unnoticed'.[13] Russia obviously did not belong to the progressive group of countries that stood for ambitious reduction targets and strict policies and measures. It argued for low obligations for the countries in transition, opposed the notion of strengthening the commitments of the Climate Convention, and asked for financial and technical assistance for JI projects. It also took a positive stance towards the inclusion of sinks in national inventories and reporting.[14]

Furthermore, Russia supported a phased approach to JI commencing with a pilot phase.[15] Taking into account its potential for CO_2 sinks, it showed interest in reforestation programmes, opening the possibility for limited sink activities to offset emissions. With the information

[12] Friedemann Müller, 'Russia and Climate Change', in Gunnar Fermann (ed.), *International Politics of Climate Change: Key Issues and Critical Actors* (Oslo: Scandinavian University Press, 1997), p. 293; Vladimir Kotov and Elena Nikitina, 'To Reduce or to Produce? Problems of Implementation of the Climate Change Convention in Russia' in J. B. Poole and R. Guthrie (eds), *Verification 1996: Arms Control, Peacekeeping and the Environment* (Boulder, CO: Westview Press, 1997), pp. 349, 357.
[13] Müller, 'Russia and Climate Change', pp. 295–6.
[14] OECD/ IEA (1996), *Climate Change Policy Initiatives: 1995/96 Update*, Vol. 2, *Selected Non-IEA Countries* (Paris: OECD/IEA), p. 115.
[15] Ibid.

obtained from a national inventory it hoped to promote projects of joint implementation on its territory.[16] The instruments favoured by the Russian Federation were regulatory and economic rather than voluntary agreements with industry or the raising of public awareness of the issue of climate change.

At COP 2 in Geneva in July 1996, Russia sided strongly with the OPEC countries. It continued both to be sceptical towards the latest scientific findings of the International Panel on Climate Change (IPCC) about human influence on climate change and to refuse to develop concrete steps to combat climate change. Oberthür argues that a factor explaining its position at this stage was the leader of the Russian delegation, Professor Israel. He became known for his peculiar arguments, which 'were apparently presented for the purpose of opposing everything'. Israel was not only sceptical about the findings of the IPCC and the previous COP decisions. At times he also argued that climate change might be positive for Russia and that mitigation measures therefore were unnecessary.[17]

Müller gives another explanation for Russia's low profile: the relationship to its major competitors regarding the export of fossil fuels, the OPEC countries, which also held a reserved position in the international climate negotiations, because of concern about the economic prospects from oil sales. According to this author, Russia

[16] Müller, 'Russia and Climate Change', pp. 294–5.
[17] Sebastian Oberthür, 'The Second Conference of the Parties', *Environmental Policy and Law*, vol. 26, no. 5, 1996, pp. 197–8; communication with Oberthür via e-mail 8 and 13 October 1998, oberthuer@ecologic.de.

did not attempt to undermine the OPEC position, which argued against strict international climate policies.[18]

Kyoto and beyond

Russia also played a rather inactive role at the negotiations at COP 3 in Kyoto in 1997. Although it is one of the major emitters, little attention seemed to be paid to its positions.[19] It was not until after the signing of the protocol that other Annex I countries fully understood the importance of Russia in the trading system that had been created, and integrated it in cooperative arrangements. Together with Ukraine, Russia had arrived in Kyoto aligning itself with the US position of stabilization of emissions at zero per cent and simply refused to negotiate on this.[20] Russia's isolation and its feeling of having been overlooked and neglected in the negotiations may partly explain the tough stance taken.

However, in general the Russian position was more in line with that of the so-called JUSSCANNZ group[21] at COP 3 (i.e. the OECD members outside the EU) than with that of its former alliance partners in OPEC. Russia, together with Ukraine and JUSSCANNZ, supported the concept of emissions trading in order to achieve

[18] Müller, 'Russia and Climate Change', p. 293.
[19] For example, John Prescott, the UK representative, did not mention Russia in his introductory speech: he put emphasis on Japan, which has considerably lower emissions.
[20] Ian Houseman et al., *Climate Change and the Energy Sector: A Country-by-country Analysis of National Programmes*, Vol. 3: The Economies in Transition (London: Financial Times, 1998).
[21] Japan/United States/Switzerland/Canada/Australia/Norway/New Zealand. Switzerland was not always aligned with the group.

greenhouse gas reductions – a matter of dispute at the Kyoto conference.[22] At first it favoured a three-gas basket (for CO_2, CH_4 and N_2O). The other three gases in question (HFCs, PFCs and SF_6) were to be addressed later.

In the course of the Kyoto negotiations Russia became a strong advocate of the so-called 'big bubble'.[23] This stands for a common reduction target for all the Annex I countries that is to be achieved individually or jointly. In the end, the Kyoto Protocol embraced the idea of a 'big bubble', and a reduction of all six gases in question by 5 per cent below the 1990 level by 2008-12 was agreed upon.

Concerning policies and measures, Russia took a midway path between, on the one hand, mandatory policies and measures to be laid down in the protocol and, on the other hand, no measures at all. For it the nature of these policies and measures depended upon the outcome of the negotiations on the basket of gases and the options for flexibility granted to the countries in transition.[24]

[22] The unfinished climate business after Kyoto' (1997), *ENDS Report*, no. 275, December, p. 19; Edward A. Smeloff, 'Global Warming: The Kyoto Protocol and Beyond', *International Policy and Law*, vol. 28, no. 2, 1998, pp. 63-8; Kristian Tangen, *Dagbok fra Kyoto: En oppsummering av forhandlingene som førte fram til Kyoto-protokollen i FNs klimakonvensjon*, FNI Report R: 007-1998 (Lysaker: Fridtjof Nansen Institute, 1998).
[23] *Earth Negotiations Bulletin* (1997), vol. 12, no. 76; 'Report of the Third Conference of the Parties to the United Nations Framework Convention on Climate Change: 1-11 December 1997' at *http://www.iisd.ca/linkages/vol12/enb1276e.html*; 'Kyoto Protocol to the United Nations Framework Convention on Climate Change' (1997), available at: *http://www.unfccc.de: Convention & Kyoto Protocol*; Müller, 'Russia and Climate Change', p. 293.
[24] *Earth Negotiations Bulletin.*

The informal alliance between JUSSCANNZ and Russia at Kyoto was strengthened by the establishment of the consultative 'Umbrella group' – Australia, Canada, Iceland, Japan, New Zealand, Norway, Russia, Ukraine, and the US – that held its first meeting in March 1998. At the meeting of the Climate Convention's subsidiary bodies in Bonn in June 1998, most of this group submitted a paper on the rules and guidelines for emissions trading. Ukraine joined the submission at a later stage.) In brief, the paper argued for a trading system with simple rules and no measures against so-called 'hot air' trading.[25] Thus within a few years Russia had made a radical change from being allied with the most reluctant parties to the climate convention to being a 'free marketer' in emissions trading, endorsing the flexibility mechanisms that could pave the way for ratification of the convention.[26]

Russia's change of position during the international negotiating process appears to conflict with important domestic sectoral interests, as it would seem to limit the development of the fuel industries. Do the 'policies and measures' adopted to combat climate change point in the same direction?

[25] UNFCCC/SB/1998/MISC.1/Add.1 and FCCC/SB/1998/MISC.1/Add.1/Rev.1; see also Kristian Tangen and Kåre Rudsar, *The Development of the Flexible Instruments in the Emerging Climate Regime*, FNI Report 1/1999 (Lysaker: Fridtjof Nansen Institute, 1999). Rumours at the Bonn conference said that a 'bubble arrangement' among the JUSSCANNZ countries and Russia and Ukraine was considered an option if the negotiations did not lead to a full-scale emissions trading system. Interviews with the participants in the Norwegian delegation.
[26] For the Kyoto Protocol to be put into force 55 countries, representing a minimum of 55 per cent of total GHG emissions, must ratify. The countries in the 'Umbrella group' represent approximately 67 per cent of world GHG emissions.

Policies and measures

According to the First National Communication several scientific and technological programmes to meet the challenges of climate change have been initiated. The general aim of these programmes is to integrate measures to regulate CO_2 emissions into the state's energy and economic policies. Increased energy efficiency in all parts of the economy enjoys the highest priority in the official *Energy Strategy of Russia,* developed in 1993-4. Further measures include structural changes in the energy supply, such as raising the share of natural gas in energy production and increasing the development and utilization of renewable energy. They also include support of technological innovation for the more efficient utilization of fossil fuels, decentralization of the energy supply system and a tax and price system providing for efficient energy use. A series of energy sub-programmes has been launched to realize these measures.[27]

It should be noted that possibly the most concrete part of these policies and programmes, i.e. everything that has to do with increasing energy efficiency and changing the relative fuel mix in the economy, is almost identical to policies which had already been adopted in the 1980s for purely economic reasons. This does not, of course, mean that such measures are irrelevant with regard to climate problems. But it could mean that the announcement of such programmes does not necessarily signify a major shift in policy and a strong political focus on climate change issues. What is important here is that there was nothing in the policies and measures

[27] First National Communication of the Russian Federation, pp. 35-6.

adopted or proposed that were in conflict with Russia's interests as a large energy-exporter. Such policies have recently been continued in, for example, the Federal Target Programme for Energy Saving 1998–2005.

In October 1996, the Russian government adopted the Federal Climate Programme on Prevention of Dangerous Climate Changes and Their Negative Consequences.[28] This programme was meant to collect together all the efforts to fulfil Russia's obligations to the climate convention. Climate measures were no longer a by-product but the explicit goal. The programme has three parts. The first is concerned with the establishment of information and monitoring systems; the second deals with adaptation measures; and the third treats 'measures to regulate emissions of greenhouse-gases into the atmosphere'.[29] It is in this part that one would expect to find trade-offs that could give a hint of the principal decisions in Russia's climate policy. However, it is difficult to find more than rather general policy goals. The instrument mentioned is investments (in energy-efficient technology). Thus again it is hard to argue that the 'new' policies and measures signify a change in overall policies. This observation is compounded by the size of the budget for the whole federal climate programme for 1997–2000. It does not amount to more than the equivalent of $40 million of which $28 million is to be covered by the federal budget.[30]

[28] *Vtoroye natsionalnoye soobschenie Rossiyskoy Federatsii* (Second National Communication of the Russian Federation) (Moscow: Interagency Commission of the Russian Federation on Climate Change Problems, 1998), p. 63.
[29] Ibid., p. 64.
[30] Ibid., p. 63.

Although the problem of inadequate financial resources caused by economic difficulties is acknowledged, the UNFCCC review team of the First National Communication criticized the lack of a 'sense of urgency' about climate mitigation measures, resulting in a lack of details on the modes and status of implementation and on the estimated impact of the various measures and programmes for climate change mitigation.[31] Concerning the lack of clear-cut instruments to implement climate policies, Russia excused itself as a country in transition, which makes it difficult to select the right instruments.[32] It seems that both the criticism and the response still pertain after the Second National Communication. For example, Russia's participation in the IPCC has remained quite limited because funding for its experts has not been made available.

The Russian Federation appears in reality to rely on the economic situation to keep emission rates at or under the 1990 level. This is also the conclusion reached by Kotov and Nikitina.[33] This implies that the prospects for greenhouse gas reductions from mitigation measures are rather dim, even if they are proposed in the national communications. The elaboration of policies and measures, i.e. programmes, in the national communications is to be interpreted instead as Russia's acceptance that a communication and an outline of policies and measures is mandatory under the UNFCCC's Art. 4.2 (a) and (b) and as the country's wish to comply with this obligation

---

[31] UNFCCC, 'Report on the In-depth Review', sec. 12 and 61.
[32] Müller, 'Russia and Climate Change', p. 293.
[33] Kotov and Nikitina, 'To Reduce or to Produce?', p. 345.

at least formally, in spite of its incapacity actually to implement these programmes.

Institutional capacity

Apart from the lack of finance, it is also questionable how far the regulatory arm of the government reaches in the implementation of energy programmes. Generally speaking, the Russian central authorities have been weakened considerably in recent years. The adoption of complex programmes requiring continuous governmental interference or control would not seem feasible in the present situation. If the authorities are not able to implement even 'no regrets' policies, little should be expected from policies that imply a trade-off between environmental and economic concerns.

In 1994 the Interagency Commission of the Russian Federation on Climate Change Problems (ICC) was established to coordinate the numerous implementation programmes. It is composed of representatives from several ministries, state committees and sectors including energy, transport, agriculture and forestry. It is headed by Rosgidromet (Hydromet), The Federal Service on Hydrometeorology and Environmental Monitoring, which also represents Russia in the International Negotiation Committee (INC). Until the 1970s Hydromet played a rather subordinate role in the Soviet Union, being responsible mainly for environmental monitoring. As environmental issues arose on the Soviet political agenda in the late 1980s, it gained importance and became the leading agency when the climate issue emerged. Clearly this agency was biased in favour of monitoring and assessments and would not be efficient in implementing policies that could mean a serious (re)distribution of benefits and burdens.

Today the ICC is considered to be a quite weak institution, with little influence even on the monitoring and control of climate-related measures. Furthermore, the responsibility for environmental monitoring is divided between Hydromet, on behalf of the ICC, and the State Committee on Environmental Protection, Goskomekologia (formerly the Ministry of Environment and Natural Resources). Müller, whose study is based on interviews with Russian experts and policy-makers, also points to the relatively low influence of the Duma on environmental policies.[34] It is quite clear that a strong institution for the implementation of policies and measures is lacking in the Russian Federation.

Public environmental concern and the influence of science

Although environmental problems were high on the political agenda in the late 1980s and formed a rallying point for political mobilization towards the end of the Soviet period, the attention of the public and the media has since shifted from environmental issues to aggravating economic problems. Among the environmental problems still being discussed, the climate issue is not very prominent. The Russian environmental NGOs' interest in the climate issue is relatively low, and they

---

[34] Müller, 'Russia and Climate Change', p. 287. See also Kotov and Nikitina, 'To Reduce or to Produce?', pp. 350–1; UNFCCC, 'Report on the In-depth Review', sec. 10.

have not exerted much influence on the country's international positioning.[35] This low interest may also be explained in part by the government's unwillingness to involve the environmental NGOs in the follow-up process of the Rio conference.[36] According to both the public and the scientific perception, the climate change problem is not an urgent environmental problem for Russia, when compared to much more immediate environmental challenges such as nuclear waste and water, air or soil pollution. Scientific advice and the need for international integration are therefore said to have a far greater influence on Russian climate policies than public concern about the environment.[37]

How stable is Russian policy?

In this chapter we have depicted the apparently dramatic change that took place in Russia's positioning in the international climate negotiations. Formerly a reluctant party that was allied with the OPEC countries, among others, and opposed to strong international measures, Russia emerged after Kyoto as a promoter of flexibility mechanisms, consulting actively within the 'Umbrella group'. On the surface this change could be interpreted as a radical reorientation of Russia's policy away from its traditional interest as a large producer and exporter of

---

[35] Kotov and Nikitina, 'To Reduce or to Produce?', p. 357.
[36] Jared E. Blumenfeld and Michelle Benedict Nowlin (eds), *One Year After Rio: Keeping the Promises of the Earth Summit: A Country-by-Country Progress Report*, 2nd edn (New York: Natural Resources Defense Council, 1993), p. 150.
[37] Müller, 'Russia and Climate Policy', pp. 285-6.

energy to a new position in which the problems created by climate change are highlighted.

This hypothesis was checked against a review of policies and measures adopted, which concluded that it was hard to identify this change in internal policy. Instead, it was argued that the policies and measures were either 'no regret' or general and vague and that they certainly did not entail any trade-off, let alone come into conflict, with energy sector interests.

Explanations of this apparent paradox – 'progressiveness' internationally but no commitment at home – may be sought partly at the institutional level. Russian politics is characterized by strong compartmentalization and poor coordination at the top. Our hypothesis is that the climate negotiations have been handled by the 'scientific' compartment and, to some extent, by the 'foreign affairs' compartment. Both have weak links to the 'economic' or 'industrial' compartments. Because of this there is no feedback from the (potentially) affected sectors.

The 'scientific' compartment, which is a section of the scientific community, is not in a position to aggregate national economic interests. In addition, the agencies developing climate policy have no real power to implement policies and measures. Because of this the policy developed is scientific in orientation, emphasizing research, monitoring and control; only to a very small extent does it include elements that would bring it into conflict with strong economic interests.

Climate policy can be understood as a function of two interrelated driving forces: societal demand and support for mitigation or adaptation measures, and the government's supply of such measures.[38] Our findings indicate that the mechanisms working on the 'supply side' of the government's climate policy are weak. Even though there are some differences between the agencies involved in climate policy development, more striking is that the climate issue is almost invisible in the confusing and crowded Russian political agenda. Neither public opinion nor parliamentary politics seems actively to have influenced the development of Russia's policy so far.

The relatively low prominence of the climate issue in Russia contrasts with the fairly clear interest structure created by the energy system, actual emissions and the fall in economic activity since the target year 1990. Nevertheless, no serious demand-side mechanisms have been detected. In all the materials and literature we have gone through, the non-participation of the energy sector in discussions about the possible impact of the climate regime is striking. As yet, no policy documents from the energy industries have been identified. The climate issue is discussed, but from a technical point of view, i.e. how the industry contributes to emissions. In other words, there has not been a demand from industry for a climate policy – as yet.

These observations lead to a natural question: how stable is Russian policy if it has been concocted within a narrow section of the administrative apparatus with few links to, or input from, society? Political parties have other concerns and environmental NGOs are very weak

---

[38] Arild Underdal (forthcoming), 'Introduction' in A. Underdal (ed.), *Modeling International Negotiations*.

in the evolving civil society in Russia, but industry is strong. The absence of industry in the development of climate policy is therefore most conspicuous. To a considerable extent, this may be explained by the traditional compartmentalization of Russian society and politics, with a long distance and large barriers between policy-making and the actors in the economic sphere, the latter having a very limited perspective on their role and responsibilities. This picture is rapidly changing, however. Today strong actors in the Russian economy would stand a good chance of influencing climate policy if they chose to do so.

This does not mean that it is easy to predict exactly in which direction industry, in particular the energy industry, would influence Russian climate policy. Russia is a big producer, consumer and exporter of energy. Given the traditional Russian or Soviet preoccupation with demand growth and output, one might expect that the energy sector would try to influence the Russian negotiating position in very much the same way as major energy producers have done elsewhere – compare the OPEC position and the lobbying of the Climate Coalition. The absence of the energy interests in policy formulation may help to explain why such positions have not been reflected strongly in Russia's position in the more recent round of negotiations.

However, the establishment of the flexibility mechanisms complicates this picture of the configuration of Russian interests. It suggests that a climate change protocol with binding targets could imply considerable economic benefits for the country. Not only the 'hot air' but also the potential for further energy-saving places Russia in a favourable position. Its potential as a seller in the international quota market and a recipient of JI investments must be accorded much weight when explaining its negotiating behaviour. The head of the Russian delegation pointed to the latter argument when he stated: 'Naturally our attitude to this idea [emissions trading] was determined to a significant extent by the understanding whereby Russia, could be one of the large potential and prospective "sellers" of emission quotas.'[39] At COP 5 in November 1999 this realization was reflected in the inclusion in the delegation of two representatives from governmental bodies dealing with foreign investment.[40]

But understanding and realizing this potential is less tangible than the traditional energy sector's interests. The country is still beset by struggles over the basic rules of the game, property rights and the division of political power. So far, the almost physically visible energy interests loom larger than the possible gains from what must be seen as a very abstract and uncertain climate regime. Hence a crucial issue becomes whether and how the energy sector can be convinced that it can benefit directly from the implementation of the Kyoto Protocol.

---

[39] A.I Bedritskiy and A.P. Metalnikov, 'Nekotorye voprosy peregovorov po ramochnoy konventsii OON ob izmenenii klimata: Ot Kioto do Buenos-Ayresa', *Energeticheskaya Politika*, no. 6, 1998, p. 23.
[40] *http://cop5.unfccc.de/listpart/lopweb.htm*

3 TRENDS IN ENERGY CONSUMPTION AND EMISSIONS

This chapter provides the general setting of Russian emissions sales. It describes both the trends that have caused the large-scale emissions reductions in Russia, and the perception of developments in the coming years. It then establishes scenarios for possible emission levels in 2010.

Russian economic and energy trends

The scope for Russia's use of the Kyoto mechanisms depends on economic trends, particularly energy consumption. The combustion of fossil fuels accounts for approximately 98 per cent of anthropogenic CO_2 emissions and 77 per cent of total greenhouse gas emissions measured in their CO_2 equivalent.[1] Consumption of energy depends, however, not only upon economic activity but also upon the efficiency of consumption. Moreover, energy efficiency is not an exogenous factor in climate policy because increasing it and thus reducing emissions is one aim of climate policy.

General economic development and the development in energy intensity are very uncertain in a country undergoing an all-encompassing economic transformation,

[1] 'The Kyoto Protocol and Russian Energy', 2nd edn (Moscow: Ministry of Fuel and Energy of the Russian Federation, Institute of Energy Strategy, 1999), p. 3.

Figure 3.1: Macroeconomic indicators and fuel consumption, 1990–9

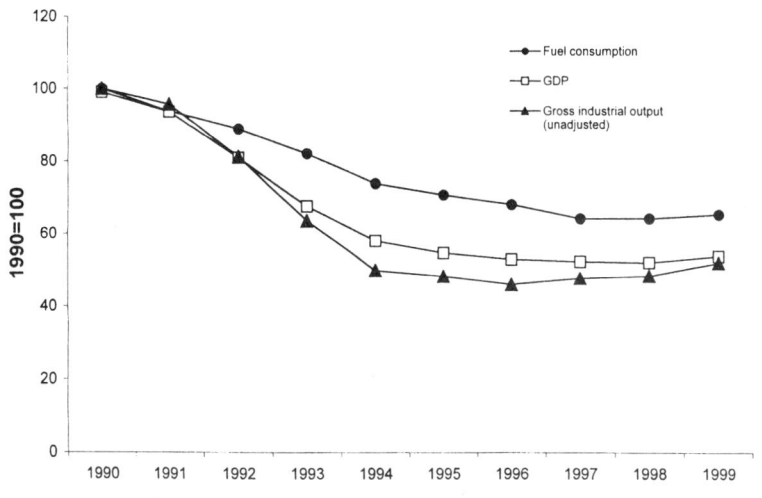

Source: *PlanEcon Report*, various issues.

and estimates of future emissions vary considerably. Forecasts are often controversial and politicized; they are important not so much for what they say as for who is saying it. Predictions of the future are closely related to an understanding of the immediate past. As perceptions will have an impact on policy, this chapter discusses as a major point the prevailing perceptions among Russian decision-makers.

Developments since 1990 have been striking, as Figure 3.1 shows. GDP and gross industrial output were halved in the course of five years and have more or less remained at that level. Total consumption of fossil fuels in 1998 was 35 per cent below the 1990 level. (Overall, however, total energy consumption is down by 30 per cent because production of nuclear- and hydro-generated electricity is down by only some 9 per cent.)[2]

The unprecedented fall in energy consumption and associated emissions reflects two main developments. First, this was the result of the dramatic economic depression following the breakdown of the centrally planned economy and the dissolution of the USSR. The reforms carried out clearly have not been sufficient to stimulate new growth. But sectoral shifts, i.e. the decline in heavy industry and the growth of the service sector, have also had an impact. Some aspects of the decline must be seen as deliberate efforts to induce sectoral changes. The heads of the Russian delegation to COPs 3, 4 and 5 list a spectrum of policies that they argue belongs to the category 'policies and measures' under the climate convention.[3] These include reductions in the military-industrial complex, with the ensuing contraction of heavy industry, liberalization of energy prices and the substitution of gas for coal in heat and power plants.

The main indicator of future emissions is the economic growth rate. The crudest estimates are based on the assumptions that the ratio of GNP to emissions is more or less constant and that the fall in economic activity is temporary. When growth resumes, energy consumption will also grow. Consequently, the 'hot air' is only a temporary phenomenon, and selling emission

[2] Figures calculated from data in *PlanEcon Energy Report*, various issues.
[3] A.I. Bedritskiy and A.P. Metalnikov, 'Nekotorye voprosy peregovorov po ramochnoy konventsii OON ob izmenenii klimata: Ot Kioto do Buenos-Ayresa', *Energeticheskaya Politika*, no. 6, 1998, p. 23.

quotas based on surplus quotas will limit Russia's economic growth potential: 'unrestrained selling of the "excess" (if it occurs on someone's will) may turn out a new bondage'.[4]

The opposing view is that Russia's economic growth will be contingent upon further sectoral changes and efficiency gains and that energy consumption will fall even if the economy grows. 'Whether or not transition to the market economy is going to be a success will greatly depend on the ability to ensure economic growth and environmental protection by improving energy efficiency.'[5] This view is also held by many foreign observers, who point to the experience of some Western countries, such as Britain in this respect, where changes between sectors as well as efficiency gains within economic sectors have enabled economic growth to occur without any significant increase in the level of emissions.

The second striking feature of the developments portrayed in Figure 3.1 is that the decline in energy and fuel consumption has been considerably less than that in economic activity. In other words, the intensity of the use of energy in the Russian economy has increased substantially from a level that was already extremely high in 1990. This means not only that the enormous energy savings potential inherent in the Soviet economy

[4] Lev Eremin (UES), 'Development of electric energy in Russia and increase in its ecological efficiency', paper presented at the workshop on 'Russian Energy Prospects and the Implications for Emissions and Climate Policy', Moscow, 15–17 September 1999, p. 27.
[5] Igor Bashmakov, 'Strengthening the Russian economy through climate change policies' (Moscow: Centre for Energy Efficiency, 1998), p. 7.

has not been realized but also that this potential has grown even larger.

The reasons for this development are several. It is understandable that in many cases the rapid contraction in economic activity does not lead to a corresponding cut in energy consumption. A huge industrial plant working at 25 per cent of capacity may need just as much energy for space heating as when working at full capacity. The lack of new investment in equipment may mean that old equipment still being used becomes increasingly energy inefficient.

Russia's political transformation is also very important. Under the Soviet regime energy was not so much sold as distributed in a system resting ultimately on political discipline. When the political basis was discarded, it was not immediately replaced by the discipline of the market economy. Even if prices were raised they did not necessarily influence consumption because consumption by the individual consumer was not always measured. (The lack of measurement has been a particular problem with regard to gas, electricity and heat consumption.)[6] The inefficiency of the price mechanism has been compounded by the non-payment crisis, which simply means that a large chunk of energy goes unpaid for. Gas and electricity have been hardest hit. In the past few years only about 20 per cent of the gas and electricity delivered to the domestic market has been paid for in cash. Another 30–40 per cent of the bills have been made up in barter and some 20–30 per cent in promissory

[6] Javier Estrada, Arild Moe and Kåre Dahl Martinsen, *The Development of European Gas Markets – Environmental, Economic and Political Perspectives* (Chichester: John Wiley & Sons, 1995), pp. 256–7.

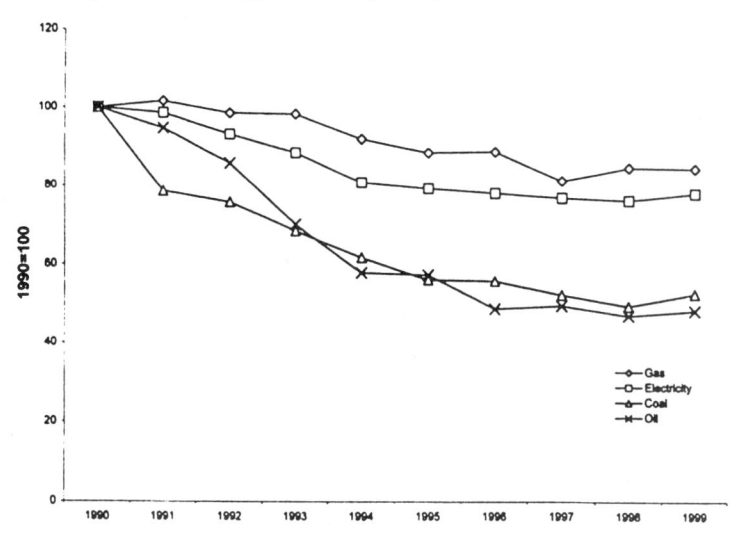

Figure 3.2: Energy consumption, 1990-9

Source: PlanEcon Energy Report, various issues.

notes and various forms of mutual cancellation of debt between enterprises. The remainder has not been paid for at all.[7]

To the extent that prices are relevant, gas and electricity prices have been held down by the authorities, making these forms of energy considerably cheaper than oil products in relative terms. This, together with the factors mentioned above, explains the development pattern shown in Figure 3.2. As can be seen, the relative fall in oil and coal consumption has greatly exceeded that of

[7] See Christiaan Vrolijk with Tobias Koch, *Russian Energy Prospects and the Implications for Emissions and Climate Policy*, Workshop Report (London: Royal Institute of International Affairs, 1999), p. 3.

gas and electricity. Whereas the fall in oil and coal usage has followed the decrease in GDP quite closely, electricity and gas demand is down only by about 20 per cent.

The prospects for gas and electricity consumption then become crucial in an assessment of future emissions. As more than 50 per cent of electricity is generated at gas-fired power plants and approximately 41 per cent of gas used domestically goes to power generation (the gas industry's own use is excluded),[8] gas will be affected twice. By 1994 gas accounted for 45 per cent of energy related CO_2 emissions, coal for 30.6 per cent and oil for 24.4 per cent.[9] Gazprom's own analyses suggest an enormous gas savings potential, but with the lack of technological as well as economic levers to control consumption, this potential cannot be realized in the foreseeable future. Therefore the official company forecasts maintain that consumption of natural gas will increase with economic growth.

Emission trends

Emission trends follow the reduction in total fuel consumption quite closely. The increasing share of gas in the fuel balance has made the drop in emissions slightly steeper. This reduced the CO_2-intensity of energy consumption by 5 per cent between 1990 and 1995.[10] Forecasts of future emissions are tightly linked to expected economic growth, and to a lesser extent to fuel mix.

[8] Gazprom, *Annual Report*, 1998; L.D. Utkina, 'Ekonomicheskie raschety effektivnosti gazoispolzovaniya', *Gazovaya Promyshlennost*, no. 6, 1999.
[9] *Vtoroye natsionalnoye soobschenie*, p. 59.
[10] Ibid., p. 87.

Russia's Second National Communication to the climate convention presents three macro-scenarios as the basis for emission forecasts: the basic scenario, the probable scenario and the optimistic scenario. Each scenario assumes that economic growth would commence in 1998. The basic scenario assumes an annual growth rate of 4 per cent when growth has picked up, whereas both the probable and optimistic scenarios assume an annual growth rate of 4.4 per cent. In the basic scenario only the cheapest and easiest energy efficiency measures are carried out, reducing the energy intensity in the economy by 0.5 per cent annually. In the probable scenario it is assumed that the government's energy efficiency programme is implemented, which will reduce energy intensity by 1.6 per cent annually. In the optimistic scenario a more extensive modernization of energy consumption is carried out, reducing energy intensity by 2 per cent annually. The expected change in the fuel mix between 1998 and 2010 is small, signifying only a 1 per cent decrease in CO_2-intensity (+2 to +4 per cent for natural gas, no change for oil, 0 to −6 per cent for coal and −2 to 0 per cent for primary electricity).

The Second National Communication does not explicitly spell out the underlying assumptions of energy consumption. However, based on the macro-assumptions quoted above, we have constructed a time series for total consumption as well as for fuel mix. Compared with actual energy consumption in 1999, the 'optimistic' variant of the emission scenarios presented in the Second National Communication entails a total growth in energy consumption by 2010 of about 45 per cent, with a 52 per cent growth for oil, 49 per cent for

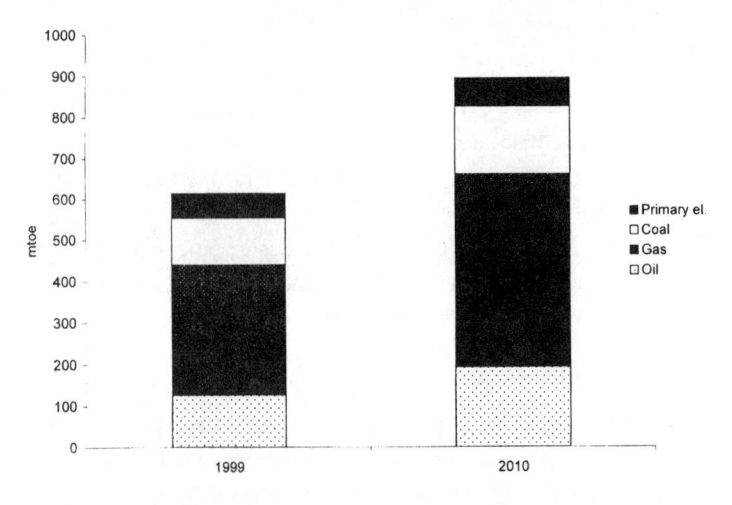

Figure 3.3: Implicit forecast of fuel consumption, 2010

Source: Author's calculations based on macro-economic forecasts in Russia's Second National Communication.

gas, 47 per cent for coal and 14 per cent for primary (hydro and nuclear) electricity (see Figure 3.3).

The emission scenarios in the Second National Communication are presented in Table 3.1. The upshot of these scenarios is that Russia will emit more CO_2 in 2010 than in 1990 if substantial energy efficiency measures are not implemented. Only in the optimistic scenario are emissions in 2010 safely below the 1990 level.

As noted in the introduction to this chapter, the official scenarios are important because they provide a point of reference for policy discussions. However, it is quite clear that the underlying assumptions about energy consumption are exaggerated, making the projected emission levels unrealistic.

Table 3.1: Total emissions, 1990 and 1994, and official emission scenarios, 2000-2010, Mt CO_2 equivalent (% 1990 level in parentheses)

	Actual	Basic	Probable	Optimistic
1990	3039			
1994	2152			
2000		2330 (77)	2280 (75)	2260 (74)
2005		2710 (89)	2570 (85)	2520 (83)
2010		3150 (104)	2910 (96)	2790 (92)

Source: Vtoroye natsionalnoye soobschenie.

Alternative scenarios

A major issue is the extent of expected economic growth. The official scenarios presented in Table 3.1 are based on a rather optimistic vision of future economic growth amounting to 3.5-4 per cent per year. Also, the spectrum of possible scenarios is rather narrow and of small variation when it comes to the underlying growth in GDP and energy intensity. It seems difficult for official representatives to present scenarios that are not based on the 'politically correct' premise that the economy will pick up soon.[11] The average annual GDP (negative) growth over the last five years has been about -2 per cent. But, as Figure 3.4 shows, the variations from year to year are large, and in 1999 growth, of 3.2 per cent was

[11] It should be noted that scenarios assuming emission growth considerably lower than the official forecasts have also been developed in Russia. See, for example, G.S. Aslanian, G.S. and V.N. Loginov, 'Protokol Kioto i perspektivy investitsionnoy aktivnosti v oblasti energoeffektivnosti v Rossii', *Energeticheskaya Politika*, no. 6, 1998, p. 29. They forecast CO_2 emissions in 2010 to be 10-15 per cent below the 1990 level.

Figure 3.4: GDP growth (%), 1990–9

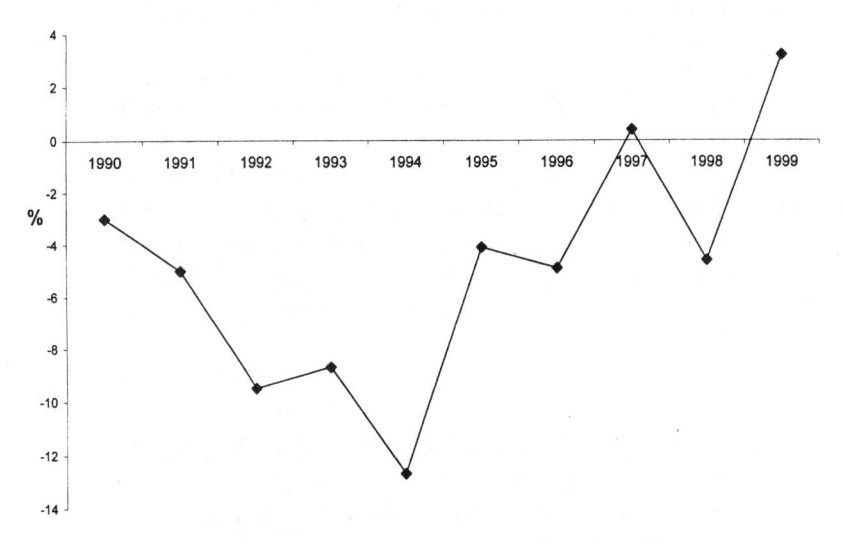

Source: PlanEcon Report, various issues.

reported for the first time in many years. Estimates for 2000 are substantially higher. So it is not unjustified to speak about an economic turnaround as assumed in the official scenarios. The question now is whether this growth is sustainable and at what level. Much of the sharp turnaround in 1999 and 2000 must be regarded as a temporary consequence of high international oil prices and delayed adjustments in domestic energy prices after the 1998 collapse. In December 1999 the domestic industrial price for natural gas was only 16.4 per cent of the export price. The average consumer price for electricity corresponded to only 1 cent per kWh.[12] In

[12] Ben Slay, 'Energy Availability: A Brake on Russia's Economic Recovery', *PlanEcon Energy Report*, May 2000.

2000 substantial price increases have already taken place or been announced.

Although the growth assumptions in the official emission scenarios are very optimistic, the expected decrease in energy intensity is very moderate. In many respects the prevalent Russian attitude is similar to that in Western Europe in 1973: economic growth and energy consumption were seen as inextricable. Improvements will of course rest on a number of factors, including investments in more efficient technology, and price reforms to induce conservation. We believe that evidence from other countries is important in this respect. Any new equipment that is installed must be expected to be much more efficient than the old equipment, hence growth in capital stock automatically entails higher energy efficiency. Because of this, higher growth may correspond to lower energy consumption than would be the case in a scenario in which growth is nil or negative, with little replacement of capital stock. In studies of the relationship between economic growth and energy efficiency in market economies, however, a so-called 'rebound' effect has been observed. This signifies that the increased efficiency which translates into reduced energy demand leads in turn to lower energy prices, which then become a stimulus for increased energy consumption in other sectors. Thus the level of energy used in the economy may remain unchanged despite increased energy efficiency in industry.[13] We believe,

---

[13] See, for example, Atle Christer Christiansen, 'Technical change and innovation in process control: Implications for process design and patterns of energy use', Working Paper (Lysaker: Fridtjof Nansen Institute, 2000).

however, that this insight has little relevance for Russia, as there is no real functioning market for energy. Energy is being paid for only partially. A development towards a functioning energy market will mean higher real prices for consumers, notwithstanding what happens with energy efficiency in industry.

Below we present three scenarios with various assumptions for economic growth, energy intensity and fuel mix. Given the fundamental uncertainties in the economic as well as the political situation in Russia, we regard each scenario as possible and also as more probable than the official scenarios. Each scenario uses 1999 data as its starting point.

Scenario 1: Restructuring and growth. We assume that the economic growth witnessed in 1999–2000 is followed by a lower, but steady 3 per cent annual growth until 2010, reflecting the restructuring of the Russian economy (see Table 3.2). The restructuring also means an annual decline in energy intensity of 2 per cent, which

Table 3.2: Restructuring and growth: assumptions and output

Assumed annual growth rate (%)		Output	(%)
GDP growth	3	Fuel used 2010 (mtoe)	744
Growth of energy intensity	-2	Oil	17
Oil	0	Gas	53
Gas	2	Coal	14
Coal	-1	Primary electricity	16
Primary electricity	0	Emissions 2010 (Mt CO_2 equivalent)	1552
		Quota surplus (%)	31

Table 3.3: Stagnation: assumptions and output

Assumed annual growth rate (%)		Output	(%)
GDP growth	0	Fuel used 2010 (mtoe)	672
Growth of energy intensity	0	Oil	19
Oil	0	Gas	47
Gas	0	Coal	17
Coal	0	Primary electricity	18
Primary electricity	0	Emissions 2010 (Mt CO_2 equivalent)	1407
		Quota surplus (%)	37

means that in 2010 it will be the same as it was in 1990. In this scenario the forces of economic growth and economic restructuring cancel each other out in terms of their impact on emissions. Thus, despite robust economic growth, the total Russian energy-related emissions in 2010 will be only 5 per cent higher than in 1999, meaning that Russia's CO_2 emissions will be 31 per cent lower than they were in 1990.

Table 3.4: Sustained decline: assumptions and output

Assumed annual growth rate (%)		Output	(%)
GDP growth	-1	Fuel used 2010 (mtoe)	635
Growth of energy intensity	0.5	Oil	18
Oil	-1	Gas	48
Gas	-0.3	Coal	16
Coal	-1	Primary electricity	19
Primary electricity	0	Emissions 2010 (Mt CO_2 equivalent)	1305
		Quota surplus (%)	42

Scenario 2: Stagnation. In this scenario, we assume that there will be zero growth and no change in the intensity of energy consumption between 1999 and 2010 (see Table 3.3). Nevertheless total CO_2 emissions will be 37 per cent lower than they were in 1990.

Scenario 3: Sustained decline. In this last scenario we assume that the economy will decline, as shown in Table 3.4, until 2010, although the decline will be much less steep than it was in 1995–8. Also, in this case the changes in energy intensity and economic growth counteract each other, but in the opposite direction from the way they do in Scenario 1. However, we assume that the impact of the former will be stronger than the latter, meaning that emissions will continue to decline. Under this scenario the emissions in 2010 will be 42 per cent lower than in 1990.

The main insight derived from these scenarios is that the quota surplus will be considerably larger than indicated by the official estimates. One main reason for this is that, as mentioned, 1999 is used as the starting point. We also see that the impact on emissions does not differ very much in the scenarios, even though assumptions for economic growth and changes in energy intensity vary considerably. Here the reason is that developments in these two variables to a large extent cancel each other out. Finally, conceivable changes in the composition of fuel use are not of a magnitude that will have a large effect on emissions.

The conclusions reached here have implications for the international negotiations as well as for domestic Russian implementation. The volume of 'hot air' will be an important issue in the international negotiations about the implementation of the Kyoto Protocol, which we discuss in the next chapter. The perception of this potential will also be essential in the development of a Russian climate policy, something we return to in Chapter 5.

4 THE EMERGING CLIMATE REGIME – CHALLENGES AND OPPORTUNITIES FOR RUSSIA

What will be Russia's piece of the quota market pie?

Chapter 3 indicated that Russia's GHG emissions in 2010 are likely to be considerably lower than those in 1990, even if no abatement measures are carried out. We found that energy-related emissions in 2010 are likely to be 30–40 per cent lower than in 1990. This estimate includes neither methane leakages nor the impact of sinks and forestry. Nevertheless, as emissions from energy consumption constitute the major share of Russian emissions, we find it likely that the above figures are representative of the development of the combined Russian emissions. This means that Russia can sell a fair amount of quotas, even if it does not carry out measures to reduce GHG emissions.

How much of the international demand for quotas Russia can meet with its quota surplus depends on the emissions growth in the other Annex I countries. The national reporting for 1995 from these countries indicates that their combined GHG emissions will exceed the 1990 level by about 18 per cent.[1] However, the moderate emission growth since 1995, particularly in the countries in economic transition, indicates that

[1] Alfsen, Holtsmark and Torvanger, *Kjøp og salg av klimagasskvoter* (Oslo: Cicero, 1998).

this estimate is too high. We believe instead that the combined growth rate in the Annex I countries, except Russia, is likely to be at about the same level as it has been for the last five years.

So far, few countries have reported emissions data for the period after 1997 to the UNFCCC. However, on the basis of the 1994-6 data and a review of various national reports, we find that an annual emission growth of about 0.6-0.8 per cent, is a reasonable estimate for the Annex I countries, again excepting Russia. Assuming that Russia's emissions will be in the range indicated in Chapter 3, its surplus quotas will meet between 35 per cent and 50 per cent of the total demand for quotas. In addition to this comes emission reduction through implementation of JI projects and other kinds of abatement projects. To what extent quotas will be generated through these projects will depend strongly on how the Russian government implements its domestic climate policy, and also on the more general investment climate in Russia, issues we shall return to later in this report.

The size of Russia's unassigned amounts of quotas is thus by any standard likely to be considerable. Whether this represents a problem for the international negotiations of climate agreements is a contested subject. The 'Umbrella group' argues that the unassigned amounts just reflect what was agreed on in Kyoto and that nothing should be done to restrict the trade. If compliance costs turn out to be low in the first commitment period, this will make it easier to agree to more ambitious targets for the next commitment periods.

Others, like Grubb,[2] warn that the presence of a large share of Russia's unassigned amounts in international trading may bring the emissions trading system into discredit. They argue that the developing countries are not likely to take on a commitment if it turns out that the Kyoto Protocol means primarily a massive transfer of money from West to East without corresponding abatement measures. Thus, the Kyoto mechanisms and the Russian quota surplus may corrupt the negotiation process and reduce the chances for achieving long-term emissions reductions.

Russia's power in the quota market

Although the size of the Russian quota surplus and the total demand for quotas is uncertain, there is little doubt that when a market has been established for emission permits, Russia, as the largest and probably the dominant supplier of emission quotas, will be an important player. In theory, if it behaved as a profit-maximizing monopoly or a member of a cartel having monopolist power, Russia would sell the volume of permits that maximized its income. That is to say, in theory it would sell the volume (Vm) that maximized the shaded area in Figure 4.1. The corresponding permit price would then be Pm.

However, although Russia's quota surplus can make it one of the most important actors in a future quota market, there are several factors that will limit its market

---

[2] Grubb et al., *The Kyoto Protocol*.

Figure 4.1: Price formation under monopoly

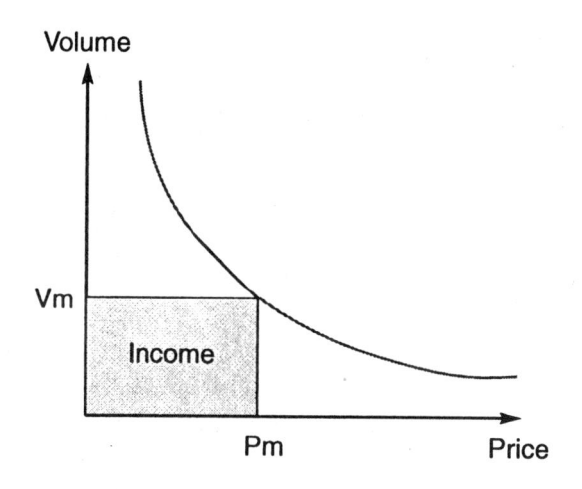

[Figure: Demand curve with axes Volume (vertical) and Price (horizontal). A shaded rectangle labelled "Income" extends from the origin to Vm on the vertical axis and Pm on the horizontal axis, bounded by the downward-sloping demand curve.]

power. First, it will not be the only supplier in the market. Of course, if the economies in transition joined forces and formed an effective cartel, it could mean considerably higher prices, as indicated by McCracken et al.[3] However, the realism of this scenario is questionable. Rather, as we shall indicate in the next chapters, it could very well happen that Russia on its own will not act as a single rational actor in the quota market. In light of this, coordinated behaviour by all the economies in transition appears unlikely. Second, it will be hard for Russia to know how much to bank in order to optimize its income. As the demand functions are at this time

---

[3] McCracken et al., 'Modeling the consequences of Kyoto', *Energy Journal*, Special Edition, 1999.

virtually unknown,[4] the permit volume that would maximize income (Vm in Figure 4.1) is almost impossible to estimate.

As a result, although its quota surplus makes Russia a powerful player, this surplus will not necessarily give it substantial market power. However, the fact that Russia has quotas to sell without having to implement measures to reduce emissions can be used to manipulate the quota price. Most other countries will have to make investments and carry out projects in order to reduce their emissions, operations that take time. The number of projects that will be carried out depends on price expectations. If Russia signals that it will sell all its surplus quotas, the expected prices will be lower than if it signals that the quotas will be banked to the next commitment period. Lower prices mean that fewer abatement projects will be carried out. If Russia, contrary to what it has signalled, decides to bank its quotas and announces this late in the first commitment period, there will be no time for implementing new projects. Quota prices will be higher than they otherwise would have been, making it possible for Russia to increase its total income.

International restrictions on emissions trading

Although there is considerable agreement between Russia and the US on the development of emissions

---

[4] Estimated quota-prices under full Annex I trading range from $5 to $50/ton CO_2. See 'Modeling the consequences of Kyoto', *Energy Journal*, Special Edition, 1999.

trading,[5] at least two strong forces in the international negotiations on the climate regime are working against the trade of the Russian surplus. First, the EU is sceptical about unlimited quota trading in general and about trading in Russian quotas in particular. Second, the developing countries are concerned with establishing an attractive clean development mechanism (CDM) and have realized that the availability of Russian quotas in the international market is likely to undercut CDM projects.

At the present stage of the climate negotiations there is a range of options for rules for the Kyoto mechanisms. How the rules are formulated and put into practice will strongly affect the price of quotas and may also modify the potential for the sale of Russian quotas. Moreover, future rules for emissions trading may influence the Russian authorities' choice of who is to be responsible for carrying out the trading.

Acquiring emissions through the flexibility mechanisms in the Kyoto Protocol is, according to the protocol text, to be 'supplementary' to domestic actions. One of the current debates in the negotiations is how this should be interpreted. In this regard, the European Union has proposed to introduce a quantitative 'cap' on the use of the mechanisms, which most of the Annex I countries outside the EU oppose.

The EU proposal introduces restrictions both on the number of quotas that may be purchased by any one

[5] In the joint statement after the summit between Bill Clinton and Vladimir Putin in June 2000 it was once again stated that 'the governments of Russia and the United States oppose the restraint of the Kyoto protocol mechanisms by quantity limits on the transfer of discharge quotas'. ITAR-TASS, 4 June 2000.

nation and on how many it may sell. The proposed caps are based on rather complicated formulas.[6] Put simply, the proposal implies that a country cannot buy or sell more quotas than an amount equivalent to approximately 5 per cent of its 1990 emissions. The EU proposal seems to stand little chance of surviving future negotiations, for several reasons. One is that the US Senate will probably refuse to ratify the Kyoto Protocol if such restrictions are introduced. However, if this proposal or other similar quantitative caps are introduced, it will obviously severely limit the potential for the sale of Russia's surplus quotas. Moreover, it will remove the incentives for Russia to introduce measures to reduce emissions, as real reductions will be given no extra value.

The rules for ensuring compliance with the Kyoto targets could also influence the potential for Russian sales. Nearly all parties participating in the international climate change negotiations seem to favour a strong compliance regime. Views differ, however, on how such a regime should be designed. One possibility would be a regime requiring compliance and reporting mechanisms at the national level to be in place before the party is allowed to participate in international emissions trading.[7] Should the negotiations turn out to specify these requirements, it could prove difficult for Russia, and maybe even more so for Ukraine,[8] to meet them. This could mean that these two countries could be suspended from

[6] See UNFCCC/SB/1999/8 for more details.
[7] Jacob Werksman, *Responding to Non-compliance Under the Climate Change Regime*, OECD Information Paper (Paris: OECD, 1998).
[8] At the time of writing Ukraine had still not reported its emissions data for 1990 to the Climate Secretariat.

international emissions trading for a period of time; it could also mean that they would not be able to enter the market until relatively late in the commitment period.

While the US and the rest of the 'Umbrella group'[9] have proposed that only sellers should be liable if the emission commitments are not complied with, the EU seems to favour shared responsibility between sellers and buyers. If such a 'buyer beware' principle is introduced, it could have a profound impact on the market structure and possibly also on how the economies in transition are likely to implement their climate policies.

Under a 'buyer beware' regime a single market price for emissions quotas will not develop, as the perceived risk of a party not meeting its commitment will be reflected in the price. For countries with an unstable political environment and low credibility among potential buyers, 'buyer beware' liability will imply reduced income from emissions trading; because their emissions will be worth less owing to the associated risk. For the economies in transition one possible measure to improve their credibility in the market would be to organize trading through bodies that are deemed reliable in the emissions market.

For Russia, this could mean those companies that are well known abroad and that already have experience in the international market place. Also, companies with assets abroad, which could serve as a form of collateral, would be desirable partners for buyers who have doubts about Russia's compliance. According to such criteria a

---

[9] See UNFCCC/SB/1999/8 for more details.

company such as, for example, Gazprom would be very well suited to handle Russian quotas. This is not to say that a system that makes the sellers liable is without problems. A seller could decide to sell even if it is not in compliance with emissions reductions if the penalty system is not credible to it. If the state in question, Russia for example, risks being penalized for the actions of private companies, it may want to centralize emissions trading strongly in one trusted, competent agency. Thus, not only the liability principle but also the more detailed penalty provisions may affect the internal organization of emissions trading.

Further, rules ensuring competition in the quota market could influence the potential for Russia's sales of surplus quotas. As argued above, Russia could hold some market power. Rules to prevent the abuse of market power are far from being finalized, but they will necessarily mean that Russia's room for manoeuvre as a unitary emissions seller will be reduced.

Conclusions

At the time of writing, the climate negotiations have been short on detailed provisions regarding the future trading regime. Thus the implications that can be drawn for economies in transition, and for Russia in particular, must be tentative. In this chapter the status of important issues arising from the negotiations, as well as the accompanying scholarly agenda, has been discussed in light of Russian interests. As should be clear, the establishment of international rules and systems for trade in emissions has an impact on the domestic 'power distribution': how rules are formulated will influence how much Russia's surplus quotas will be traded and who is going to trade them.

It is argued that Russia's surplus quotas will not necessarily become 'internationally tradable surplus quotas', i.e. Russia may be forced, or decide on its own initiative to keep all or part of its surplus outside international emissions trading. There are internal as well as external forces that work in this direction. Also, traditional monopolist theory indicates that it could be profitable for Russia not to sell all its surplus quotas. But when selling them, there are good reasons for centralizing their sale with a commercial actor which is well known abroad and has the relevant experience.

5 DOMESTIC RUSSIAN IMPLEMENTATION

This chapter explores possible ways in which Russia might implement a climate policy with emphasis on the flexibility mechanisms of the Kyoto Protocol. It then discusses what appears to be Russia's most likely course of action against the background of the interests of the relevant domestic actors and the institutional framework in which they operate. To do this, it assesses who the most likely actors are, their interests and their powers.

In formulating a climate policy, the Russian government is faced with two interlinked questions: what should be done with the surplus quotas, and what kind of instrument, if any, should be applied domestically?

A rational and economically efficient policy with the goal of maximizing Russia's welfare would probably mean that it would behave as a monopolist or a cartel member when selling quotas abroad (see Chapter 4) and introduce environmental taxes or tradable quotas domestically. But as we shall argue below, what appears rational from a Western point of view will not necessarily be implemented in Russia. Its position raises a special set of policy questions regarding the balance between the flexibility mechanisms.

What is at stake?

From the outset the governments party to the Kyoto Protocol hold the quotas assigned to them under the agreement. The governments may then choose to reallocate these quotas to commercial entities. The point of departure for this part of our analysis is to establish what values and interests are at stake and if there is a (potential) conflict in Russia over the distribution of gains from implementing the protocol.

Discussion about the distribution of gains is not unique to Russia. In all the Annex I countries the implementation of the protocol entails a distribution of burdens and gains. For example, in countries setting up an emissions trading system the question of the initial distribution of quotas among various national actors will have to be addressed. In these countries the main focus is on how to distribute the burden in a way that is fair and that has favourable implications for the level of emissions. However, what matters in a competitive system is the relative position. Therefore, to achieve a lower burden than that imposed on competitors can also be conceived of as a net gain.

Russia's special situation is that it is likely to be a net receiver of funds from the implementation of the two relevant flexibility mechanisms in the Kyoto Protocol, joint implementation and emissions trading. Thus the possible gains for the country are quite clear: the transfer of resources either in the form of cash with no strings attached or as investments in emissions-reduction measures with substantial positive externalities.

Theoretically, gains can accrue at a national as well as a sub-national level, with some important differences between emissions trading and JI, a matter to which we shall return below. The government could centralize all transactions and make sure that the benefits are distributed further in an economically optimal way for the country. But transactions could also be decentralized to sub-national actors such as companies, providing them with the opportunity to receive the gains directly.

It is more difficult to identify possible losses from the implementation of the Kyoto mechanisms, i.e. the transfer of assigned amounts from Russia to other countries. But, as mentioned in Chapter 3, it is argued in Russia that an 'uncontrolled' sale of assigned amounts could put a cap on Russian economic growth and be seen as detrimental to the welfare of the country at large. Thus there are at least perceived negative effects. Such potential losses accrue primarily at the national level. If possible limitations on economic activity are distributed evenly throughout the economy, they will not have a particular effect on any one sub-national actor.

Because of Russia's very favourable position with regard to emissions, policy measures that would impose net burdens on any sub-national actor seem unlikely. All measures discussed in any detail in the official documents seem to be 'no-regrets policies'.[1] Thus, unlike Western industrial sectors or individual companies, Russian businesses, to the extent that they are aware of the issue at all, are concerned about their share of the benefits and not the potential losses.

[1] *Vtoroye natsionalnoye soobschenie*, pp. 65–82.

For this dichotomous set of actors, national versus sub-national, the imbalance between gains and losses has implications with regard to their preferences. Clearly each level would prefer an institutional arrangement whose benefits accrue on its own level. One would expect the central authorities to prefer mechanisms that leave the gains at their disposal, just as one would suppose that the sub-national actors would work towards the opposite objective. And because the possible losses accrue primarily at the state level, it could logically be argued that they must be balanced against gains at that level.

But, as already indicated, the gains are much more tangible than the potential losses. Even if one needs to be aware of the 'loss' argument stated above, the most relevant perspective for analysing the implementation issue is to look at it as a distribution of gains. In other words, who gains what? With this as a starting point we shall look more closely at the actors involved.

Who are the actors?

Russia and the unitary actor model

In the analysis in Chapters 3 and 4 we treated Russia as essentially a unitary actor. This common simplifying assumption is, as always, easy to attack, but it has provided us at least with a point of reference for the subsequent discussion of sub-national actors and their interests. However, special caution is required when Russia is subjected to the unitary rational actor model. The Soviet system has left an imprint on the analysis of Russia today that must be taken into account. The Soviet system presupposed a degree of central, rational authority that made the unitary rational actor model seem not only a simplifying assumption but also something close to reality. This view was compounded by the limited flow of information, which overstated the role of the central authorities. There is a tendency to continue with this framework of analysis for Russia today, more so than for other states, even though the changes in the country as well as available information do not warrant it.

The relevance of this model has been undermined by three developments. The first is the evolution of a federal state structure. A leading foreign analyst of Russia sums up the present status thus:

> the growing weakness of the federal centre and its failure to meet the expectations once vested in it have had several longer-term consequences. They have multiplied the conflicts between centre and periphery over jurisdictional and distributive issues. They have also contributed to a shift in focus ... to one of seeking regional strategies for survival as more self-sufficient entities.[2]

Second, the competition and conflict among various federal government agencies have reached proportions beyond the skirmishes envisaged in the 'bureaucratic politics' model. For ministries publicly to hold opposing views on important policy issues occurs so frequently that no special notice is taken. Third, the transfer of power to private citizens and corporations[3] without an

[2] Gail Lapidus, 'Asymmetrical Federalism and State Breakdown in Russia', *Post-Soviet Affairs*, vol. 15, January–March 1999, pp. 74–82.
[3] See discussion of corporatism in A. Moe and V. Kryukov, *The New Russian Corporatism: A Case Study of Gazprom* (London: Royal Institute of International Affairs, 1996).

accompanying legal framework also raises serious questions about the power and role of the central government in many issues.

President Vladimir Putin clearly aims to strengthen the central authorities in Russia by curbing the power of regional authorities, and by establishing a framework that would also reduce corporate power. If he succeeds, the power balance will change somewhat, but we find it unlikely that it will be altered fundamentally. It also seems unlikely that a stable balance is soon to be achieved. Thus, major policies will continue to be worked out in some kind of understanding with the regions as well as the corporations.

As shown in Chapter 2, participation in the development of Russia's climate policy has been narrow, and to some extent Russia can be conceived of as a unitary actor in this process. The low prominence of the issue was pointed to as an explanation for this. Therefore, when we criticize the use of the rational unitary actor model in this study of the implementation of the climate regime in Russia, we also have in mind *emerging* and *potential* actors. According to the official statement of Russia's head of delegation at COP 5 in November 1999, 'In Russia the interest of ministries, agencies, state and private industrial enterprises for the organizational and legal parameters [of the flexibility mechanisms] is growing'.[4] This statement corresponds well with a rapidly increasing number of reports and articles about these issues published since Kyoto.

---

[4] A. I. Bedritskiy, 'Zayavlenie' (statement), High-level segment, COP 5, Bonn, 2 November 1999.

Basic preferences

Beginning with the federal level, the lack of an overriding integrated approach to climate policies has already been noted. The various government agencies are either tied to a sub-national constituency or they are themselves operating as sub-national actors. Moreover, they have little faith that any other agency can develop and implement a policy that would benefit the country as a whole. Thus they will logically incline towards arrangements that leave control over implementation in their own hands.

The main agencies involved in implementation fall into two main categories.[5] One section has been headed by the State Committee for Environmental Protection – Goskomekologiya. It has formulated an overall emissions management policy, and its regional committees have implemented that policy. Other state agencies have provided input: the Ministry of Fuel and Energy, the Russian Forestry Committee and the Ministry of Transport. These agencies also formulate emission control policies within their own sectors. The Ministry of Economy is responsible for macroeconomic forecasts. In May 2000 the Russian government dissolved Goskomekologiya. Some of its functions will be transferred to the Ministry of Natural Resources, but it is not yet clear who will handle emission policy. The second part of the

[5] S. Kuraev, S. Markin and E. Strukova , 'Domestic Regulation of Greenhouse Gases and Problems of Initial Allocation of Emission Quotas', paper presented at Bilateral Workshop on US–Russian Greenhouse Gas Emissions Trading, organized by the Harvard Institute for International Development and USAID, Moscow, 1–2 July 1998.

structure is responsible for greenhouse gas emissions control. The superior body here is the Russian Federal Service for Hydrometeorology and Environmental Monitoring – Rosgidromet or Hydromet. The Interagency Commission of the Russian Federation on Climate Change Problems, headed by Hydromet, has been responsible hitherto for the certification, licensing and registration of JI projects in their pilot phase. The Ministry of Finance is responsible for distributing the revenues and finances from the implementation of the state climate change policy.[6]

This structure seems quite logical but the impression is that authority is not clearly defined and that there is an underlying conflict among these agencies. The key problems are those connected to the certification and licensing of quota transfers. Besides differences in institutional viewpoints, this conflict may also have material elements, as agencies that handle transactions are likely to benefit economically too, a widespread practice in Russian administration.

Even though climate policies are not at the forefront in any of the agencies mentioned above, they all have special departments, or at least officials, devoted to the climate issue. The impression is that the attention given to the issue has increased considerably after the Kyoto conference. According to Koch and Michaelowa,[7] Goskomekologiya and the Ministry of Fuel and Energy 'developed an interest in taking over the initiative' from Hydromet,

[6] Ibid.
[7] Tobias Koch and Axel Michaelowa, 'Hot air reduction for Russia through measures prior to 2008 and non-quantifiable projects' (Moscow: Centre for Energy Policy, 1999).

which has been the dominant agency since the emergence of the GHG issue (see Chapter 2).

The regional level has generally increased in importance, but initiatives to make the regional administrative level an actor in the implementation of the flexibility mechanisms have not yet been identified.[8] Nevertheless, one should not rule out such initiatives, particularly if the sale of surplus quotas becomes a reality. Regional administrations are *potential* players.

The third main group of actors is, of course, industry or business. Some Russian enterprises have already been involved in AIJ (activities implemented jointly) projects.[9] The benefits for companies involved in such projects are very tangible. The investments that the foreign partner brings in to reduce greenhouse gas emissions have strong positive side effects because they usually involve the modernization of plant. The number of enterprises interested in such projects must be expected to increase as information spreads and the period for implementation of 'real' JI projects approaches.

These three groups or levels of actors possess different forms of power:

- The agencies on the federal level formulate the rules and may administer them; they may also have a position as a certifier of transactions: in other words,

---

[8] No written sources indicate such a development; neither do interviews with officials in the central agencies (September and November 1999) reveal information about any initiatives.

[9] As of September 2000, nine AIJ projects were under implementation in Russia. For a list of projects see http://www.unfccc.int/program/aij/aijproj.html.

they determine who is going to participate directly in the implementation.

- The industry level is where the results of implementation will be directly felt, where emission cuts must be made and the actual physical measures undertaken.
- The regional administrative level has elements of both. It may try to acquire a rule-making or certifying role, but it is also closely linked to organizations and enterprises where emission cuts must be made, such as district heating and regional electricity and gas networks. The regional administrations would also benefit directly if energy efficiency projects could lift some of the heavy burden they carry in terms of energy subsidies. Subsidies of electricity and heat supplies typically absorb 25-40 per cent of their budgets.[10]

One would expect that the level controlling the rules would prefer emissions trading, as it provides the most flexibility and efficiency. Many analysts have pointed this out,[11] and potential importers of assigned amounts have done much to provide Russia with training and insight into emissions trading.[12]

Conversely, one would expect actors with direct links

[10] Igor Bashmakov, 'Strengthening the Russian Economy Through Climate Change Policies' (Moscow: Centre for Energy Efficiency, 1998).
[11] For an overview of the literature see Kristian Tangen and Kåre Rudsar, *The Development of the Flexible Instruments in the Emerging Climate Regime*, FNI-report 1/1999 (Lysaker: Fridtjof Nansen Institute, 1999).
[12] This has taken the form of several seminars organized by US agencies in Russia, as well as the training of selected Russian specialists in the US.

to emitters to be more inclined towards joint implementation, because they are more likely to be affected directly by the positive secondary effects of JI projects, such as increased efficiency and the transfer of know-how, than towards emissions trading. In addition it may be argued that investments in joint implementation projects are likely to be combined with other purely commercial investments in the Russian economy by foreign companies. JI can be regarded as an additional stimulus to invest. This further increases the potential value of this flexibility mechanism.

On paper, emissions trading can yield the same benefits with regard to emission reduction as JI, but at a lower cost. If the state sells quotas, it can direct the income into investments in abatement or modernization projects in which the pay-off will be largest. With emissions trading the institutional arrangement is also simpler, thereby reducing the transaction costs compared to JI, in which various certification procedures must be used and baselines for individual projects worked out. Emissions trading with quotas obtained from energy efficiency improvements clearly enjoys support from specialists and agencies concerned with energy efficiency.[13]

However, the smooth operation of such a system presupposes transparent political procedures and political controls ensuring that investments are actually channelled into emission reduction. It also presupposes the existence of a developed market economy that can

[13] 'The Kyoto Protocol and Russian Energy', p. 6.

generate comparable information about costs for alternative emission reduction projects. Neither of these conditions is fulfilled today, and neither is likely to be fulfilled in the near future. In addition, the prevailing crisis in state finances in Russia makes it difficult to set aside investment funds when there are so many other problems that need to be solved. The upshot is that agencies genuinely interested in facilitating emission reductions and/or increasing energy efficiency have good reason to be concerned that adoption of emissions trading will not yield the results they want.[14]

JI is a more cumbersome mechanism. It is more decentralized because projects must be negotiated directly with the emitters, but various certification and control functions may nevertheless remain subject to central control. As argued above, it is not so strange that sub-actors at the enterprise or regional level more easily recognize the benefits for themselves in the use of this mechanism. The main point here is that owing to the imperfections of the political and economic system, joint implementation also finds strong support at the central level.

The debate over surplus quotas

The surplus quotas or 'hot air' complicate the analysis of implementation and are a controversial issue both internationally and domestically. Leaving aside the international reservations or attempts to limit trade in surplus

[14] See, for example, Ilya Popov, 'Results of the Kyoto Conference: Failure or Success?', *Bulletin of the Centre for Russian Environmental Policy*, no. 3, June 1998.

quotas, we shall look at how this issue may be treated in Russia and how it may affect the various actors.

One option for handling surplus quotas would be for the Russian government to sell them, in whole or in part, to foreign actors with no further obligations for the buyer. The point with such a strategy would be to generate foreign currency earnings for the state much like the export of a commodity over which the state holds a monopoly. One variant of such a plain sale strategy would be to use the sale of the quotas to offset Russia's debt to foreign countries. It has been suggested that this is one option that has been under consideration by the Clinton administration.[15]

If a sale strategy is chosen, leaving the sales operations to others will probably be profitable. The international market for climate quotas is likely to be, particularly in its early phase, highly volatile. Maximizing income from large-scale sales of quotas thus requires considerable know-how. For the Russian government this would be an argument for leaving the sales operations to foreign brokers, for example, or to domestic actors possessing the relevant experience.

If surplus quotas are regarded only as an instrument to generate additional revenue for Russia, parallels may be drawn with the quota and licensing systems which have been employed for raw materials and commodities. Apart from the quotas given to the producers, export quotas

[15] Workshop on 'Russian Energy Prospects and the Implications for Emissions and Climate Policy', Moscow, October 1999. Other similar schemes can also be foreseen, i.e. quotas in return for concessions in other policy areas or as barter for commodities.

have also been distributed to a wide range of entities without any connection to the raw material or commodity. This has simply been another way of handing out government subsidies without going the more cumbersome way of collecting taxes and passing budgets through parliament. Even if this practice has been reduced relative to the early and mid 1990s, it would seem tempting for the government to return to this system, especially when the good in question, surplus quotas, is basically free.

A different variant of selling the surplus quotas would be to require that those receiving quotas invest in abatement measures in Russia. One might think that in order for this to make sense, foreign participation must comprise more than the transfer of economic resources. It would have to involve technology transfer, otherwise the Russian government could invest the proceeds from quota sales itself. Used as a lever for investments, such a scheme could be implemented in several ways. It could use the JI methodology as a point of departure and calculate the number of quotas to be transferred on the basis of the reductions achieved from concrete projects. However, as long as quotas (assigned amounts), not JI certificates, are given in return for projects, it is up to the Russian government to determine how many quotas should be transferred. It can choose to give quotas for reductions that take place before the Kyoto period, i.e. before 2008, or only for reductions in the Kyoto period (2008–12). The former is what often has been referred to as 'early crediting'.[16]

[16] Note, for example, Matthew Varilek and Christiaan Vrolijk, *Emissions Trading and Early Crediting*, Workshop Report (London: Royal Institute of International Affairs, 1999).

Russia will also have to decide whether it will compensate reductions on a one-to-one basis or whether it will give the investor fewer or more quotas than the equivalent reduction estimated for the project. Thus, in the last resort it will be a matter of negotiation between the Russian governmental bodies and the investor over how many quotas the investor will receive.

In principle, sales of surplus quotas could also be tied to the introduction of a domestic system for emissions trading in Russia. In such a system commercial entities could trade the quotas using the same model that is planned in several Western countries. Currently, the idea of establishing a domestic system for emissions trading seems far from becoming a reality in Russia. This relates to the general problems of making the market economy work. Furthermore, the current climate policy is focused on programmes that have little or no similarity to quota trading (see Chapter 2).

However, if other countries implement domestic quota systems and allocate quotas to industry by so-called 'grandfathering',[17] Russian actors could start lobbying for similar schemes. A system in which quotas are freely allocated to Russian actors on the basis of their 1990 emissions, for example, would mean a massive transfer of capital from the state to industry. Consequently, many actors might then favour a system for domestic trading tied to the international quota market.

While a system for domestic emissions trading connected to the international market for quotas could link

[17] Under 'grandfathering' the quotas are allocated to private actors for free, usually on the basis of historical emissions rates.

sales of surplus quotas with the introduction of climate instruments in Russia, other policy measures could also be introduced. As described in Chapter 2, various energy efficiency programmes dominate Russia's climate policy. The extent of their real impact on energy use is uncertain. However, in a situation in which the sale of quotas provides a source of income for the state, strengthening these programmes could become attractive.

Taxing emissions is theoretically also an option. It would be a more effective way to reduce emissions than today's command-and-control programmes. But in general, taxation is a dubious instrument because of the inadequacy of market mechanisms in Russia and the overwhelming non-payment problem in the Russian economy. General GHG taxes could also be politically difficult to introduce owing to increased household costs and resistance to closing down emissions-intensive industries. However, despite these general reservations, the climate issue might become a reason for the government to introduce new taxes for selected companies or sectors at a later stage, something we return to in Chapters 6 and 7.

In Chapter 3 we presented the not uncommon Russian viewpoint that 'hot air' should not be sold but kept as a 'reserve' in order to avoid limitations on economic growth and accompanying energy consumption in the future. Keeping this reserve is possible as the Kyoto Protocol approves so-called 'banking'; i.e. quotas not used in one commitment period can be saved and used later. The larger the potential is for surplus quotas, the more difficult it is to sustain the 'reserve' argument. The volumes estimated in Chapter 3 could permit the 'banking' of large amounts and still give room for sales. But, as long as there is strong disagreement about the size of surplus quotas, the 'reserve' argument is likely to carry considerable weight.

However, there is also a narrower debate going on about surplus quotas among those who have no time for the 'reserve' argument. The argument against 'hot air' is, they maintain, based on a widespread lack of confidence in the state's ability to manage financial resources in a rational way. According to this view income from surplus quotas sales will probably be squandered, and in the best case it will be used for purposes that have nothing to do with the environment or gains in efficiency.[18] A counter-argument to this line of reasoning is that even if revenues are used for other purposes, these purposes may be of higher priority than energy efficiency.

A strong argument against the sale of surplus quotas is that their availability on the international emissions quota market will prevent JI in Russia with all its positive side-effects. The sale of surplus quotas will postpone external investment until the quotas are used up, at which point Russia will find itself with basically the same inefficient energy consumption structure as when trading started. Others hold that it will indeed be possible to construct mechanisms that allow for a transfer of resources from the sale of surplus quotas to efficiency measures, as outlined above, and that the sale of unassigned amounts will provide Russia with important liquidity for such measures sooner than if surplus quotas sales were abolished.[19]

[18] See Koch and Michaelowa, 'Hot air reduction for Russia'.
[19] A. A. Golub, Ye. B. Strukova and A. A. Averchenkova, 'Ekonomicheskie osnovy torgovli kvotami na vybrosy parnikovykh gazov', *Energeticheskaya Politika*, no. 6, 1998, pp. 52–3.

The controversy over surplus quotas in Russia is not likely to be resolved very soon. And also it may be asked whether there may be side benefits that can be brought into the discussion. In other words, could surplus quotas be sold in a way that would bring benefits in addition to revenue?

'Implementation games'

In most of the countries in Annex I to the Kyoto Protocol the 'battle' over implementation of the protocol is between economic sectors, industrial sectors or individual companies trying to minimize the burden they expect from emission cuts. They work to minimize the direct impact on themselves or at least to ensure that their relative position *vis-à-vis* competitors is not harmed.

This framework for understanding the (potential) behaviour of Russian actors does not fit the situation completely. We would argue that for the foreseeable future the main issue is about how best to derive side benefits from the implementation of the Kyoto mechanisms. With 'hot air' as a buffer it is almost impossible to imagine that the Russian authorities would be interested in or possess the means for enforcing a policy to achieve further emission cuts by way of negative sanctions such as emission taxes. The only possible way is to use the flexibility mechanisms and entice emitters to cut emissions by offering them rewards. Conversely, only actors with a very long-term perspective would take into account today the possibility of enforced emission cuts in the future. Thus the reason to 'participate in implementation' is not to avoid costs but to enjoy the possibility of receiving investments with many positive side effects more or less without cost.

The Rusisan 'battle' over implementation can be construed as a series of implicit games. Two 'meta-games' partly overlap: one concerns participation in the decision-making process for implementation policy and the other concerns the choice of flexibility mechanism(s) and the basic rules for their implementation.

The first game is between the central authorities and various sub-national actors. The starting point for the central authorities is quite clear. In the words of the Ministry of Fuel and Energy's leading climate change officials:

> In Russia, there is not and will not be in the near future organizational conditions for 'distribution' of quotas between regions, as well as between enterprises and companies in the energy sector, in such a manner as will probably be done in many developed countries. In the foreseeable future, the state will act in all capacities on the 'climate arena' in the realization of pilot projects, carry responsibility towards the international community for the fulfilment of obligations, organization of monitoring, trading (transfer of quotas) and so on. While in the longer perspective, evidently, a decentralization of the process is possible, at least in the period of 'early trading' there are no alternatives to the given scheme.[20]

But, as argued above, we find it inconceivable that the central authorities will be able to retain exclusive control

---

[20] A. M. Mastepanov and O. B. Plyuzhnikov, 'Energetika posle Kioto', *Energeticheskaya Politika*, no. 6, p. 16, 1998.

of implementation. When information about the opportunities embedded in the Kyoto mechanisms spreads, many new actors on the sub-national level are likely to emerge and claim a role in the development of Russian policy. This development is, in fact, almost anticipated in the quotation above. Thus we expect the outcome of this game to follow the general thrust of politico-economic developments in Russia: there will be a mixed result, which will enable the participation of both central and sub-national actors. But the exact rules and weight of the various levels and participants are likely to be adjusted over time. This would parallel other processes in Russia, in which rules and power change constantly.

The second game is about the choice of flexibility mechanism. Three outcomes are possible: JI, ET or both. Most of the new participants in the first game will favour JI, as few of them will have much chance of participating in emissions trading. Thus it seems certain that JI will be given a strong place in Russia's implementation policy. For the same reason it is quite inconceivable that Russia will go for ET exclusively. But we find it quite probable that a certain level of ET will be included, although it is difficult to say how much. Even those who favour JI in principle argue that because of the special problems of the transition economy, in many cases it may be very difficult to form the baselines required for JI projects. In such cases ET might be used as a substitute.[21] Nevertheless, the most important conclusion here is that joint implementation or other variants of project-based instruments are likely to play an important role.

[21] 'The Kyoto Protocol and Russian Energy', p. 6.

An interesting upshot of this discussion is that the rather large 'community' which sees a potential in joint implementation may perceive a threat from surplus quotas sales. If sales of surplus quotas are launched on a large scale, they may destroy the potential for JI projects with all their positive side effects. Thus industry may come out against surplus quotas, at least as long as it enjoys a privileged position with regard to such quotas, e.g. obtaining them for free.

This brings us to a third set of games, which concerns actual participation in JI projects and ET. Even though joint implementation projects 'produce' their own transferable quotas or ERUs (emission reduction units), the number of projects will influence the international market price for quotas and also the terms of each individual JI project. If JI is unleashed on a large scale in Russia, foreign investors are likely to shop around for those projects that give them the most ERUs for their money. Because of the size and inefficiency of the Russian economy, we find it likely that Russia will provide a very large share of the market for JI projects internationally. Thus an oversupply of projects will mean that Russian projects will compete primarily with other Russian projects. This is a strong argument for some sort of central selection mechanism.

As is apparent from the discussion earlier in this chapter, we rule out the possibility that the selection of JI projects will be a rational decision-making process. Even if some central agency retained control of this selection, which we have concluded is not likely, the conditions are not in place for rational decisions, i.e. selection of JI projects that maximize the benefits for the country as a whole. There are too many uncertainties about the effects of various projects, and the market mechanism is too poorly developed to make comparison of projects a certain venture.

Many actors are likely to claim their rightful access to the benefits of the flexibility mechanisms. They will compete with each other in what is essentially a variable-sum game. We see this as a game involving mainly various sub-national actors but links to central authorities and support from them will be an essential resource for successful competition (see below).

The outcome of this game or set of games will also depend on other factors. Information, i.e. knowledge about the mechanisms and an understanding of their potential, is clearly an essential resource. The earlier an actor acquires information, the better chance it stands to gain a good position in the implementation phase. An indication of the degree of preparedness is the establishment of emission inventories. By March 1999, it was reported that Lukoil, the Tyumen Oil Company and Gazprom were preparing inventories.[22] The state-owned holding company for the electricity sector, United Energy Systems of Russia, had already carried out an inventory of CO_2 emissions from all power plants and boilers in the electricity sector in 1998-9.[23]

A second valuable resource is the ability to handle a JI project, i.e. to work out plans and manage investments

[22] Ibid., p. 12.
[23] Eremin, 'Development of electric energy in Russia' (see ch. 3, n. 4 above), p. 4.

in such a manner as to convince the foreign partner. Such resources are very unevenly distributed. Large companies which are used to dealing with foreign partners and which have experience in project financing will clearly be ahead. The same argument is valid for quota trading if it will be directly connected to emission cuts.

Thus we argue that the uneven distribution of relevant resources will significantly reduce the potential number of participants in JI and ET, at least early on. However, as alluded to above, apart from the 'internal' resources possessed by each individual actor, its relationship with the central authorities will also be important. Even though access to JI will be decentralized in principle, it is still likely that some central body or bodies will influence the selection of projects or, in other words, pick the final winners from the group of actors which have come out on top in the game depicted above. As mentioned earlier, some enterprises maintain very strong links with the central authorities and are more important than others in their eyes. Therefore these authorities may judge that giving the more important actors access to JI is better than giving it to others. This point is even clearer if one envisages emissions trading involving 'reinvestment of trading benefits' on a project basis. In this case the crucial issue becomes the initial distribution of quotas. But whose quotas should be sold will require the same deliberations as for selecting JI projects. Thus, this game is likely to be very much a political process in which economic arguments are used. Arguments are likely to centre upon the individual enterprise's or project's significance for the Russian economy.

However, one should not rule out a certain amount of rationality in this process either. Even if the tools to measure efficiency and benefits are underdeveloped and crude, it could be that some projects have such striking features that their benefits to the country as a whole stand out in comparison with others. For example, if a project could increase Russia's exports and foreign currency income as well as reduce emissions and modernize plant, would it not be rational to select it?

Here it should be noted that under certain circumstances emissions could be regarded more as an asset than a liability. As argued earlier, there is little or no risk that a company will face emission taxes that can become a burden. On the contrary, emissions can be a source of income. Easily reducible emissions can be converted into quotas, which can give a resource rent very similar to income from surplus quotas. From this it follows that actors will want to extend their operations to include activities that generate GHG emissions if they believe that they can convert these emissions into valuable JI projects at a later date, or even sell quotas. Because of the non-transparency of the Russian economy it is very difficult to tax this 'resource'. It is difficult to determine the costs of reducing emissions, and a company has every reason and possibility to manipulate costs to show that these are high and that consequently there is little or no profit from transferring quotas. Companies that have large emissions may enter into negotiations with the authorities about the selection of projects. A company that has many cheap emission reduction possibilities will have a better negotiating position than others, because it can offer the government a larger share of the gains and still be well off itself.

The large energy companies clearly stand out with regard to the resources discussed above and are likely to become important players in the implementation of Russia's climate policies. They have the relevant experience and institutional support, and some already possess a significant insight into the climate issue. They also control a very large share of emissions through their own operations. In addition they have a potential strong influence over final consumers, many of whom are heavily indebted to the energy suppliers. These relationships could make it possible for energy companies to swap debt for emissions if they deem control over emissions to be an asset.

In the next chapter we take a closer look at the most important company in this regard: the gas company Gazprom.

6 GAZPROM – A KEY ACTOR

The purpose of this chapter is to analyse the Russian gas company Gazprom with a view to understanding whether it can and will get a role in Russia's implementation of the Kyoto Protocol along the lines described in Chapter 5. We survey briefly Gazprom's part in supplying Russia's energy and in the economy in general and then give a picture of emissions emanating from the gas sector. The company's export strategy is examined in search of relevant lessons for future quota trading and the prospects for change in the gas sector are discussed. A concluding section sums up the gas industry's strength with regard to a role in Russia's implementation of the Kyoto Protocol.

Gazprom in the Russian economy

Gazprom has a unique position in Russia in terms of its size and importance in supplying energy and as a hard currency earner. Gazprom is responsible for approximately 94 per cent of annual national gas production and supplies more than 50 per cent of the primary energy consumed in Russia. Its gross annual hard currency earnings are about $8 billion.[1] About half of this is channelled into state coffers; it represents 15 per cent of

[1] Calculated on the basis of data in Gazprom, *Godovoy otschet (Annual Report)*, 1998 and *PlanEcon Energy Report*, April 1999.

Russia's hard currency earnings,[2] making Gazprom its most important hard currency earner, and also overshadows the total state revenue from oil exports. At the same time the company contributes 25 per cent of collected taxes in Russia.[3] It is the largest gas company in the world, accounting for one-quarter of world production, and is also the world's largest gas exporter.

Of Russia's domestic gas consumption, 40 per cent goes to electricity generation. Industry accounts for 27 per cent while the communal sector consumes only 16 per cent. Various other consumers take up the remaining 17 per cent.

The operation of distribution pipelines and deliveries to final consumers has traditioinally not been part of Gazprom's tasks. It operates the trunk pipeline system and sells its gas to regional distribution companies owned mainly by regional and municipal authorities.[4] However, over the past few years Gazprom has given domestic operations a more commercial focus; it has introduced direct contracts with large end-consumers who can be served more or less directly from the trunk pipelines, bypassing the networks. As a result of these steps, by the beginning of 1999 Gazprom was supplying almost 20 per cent of gas on the domestic market

[2] Jonathan Stern, 'Soviet and Russian Gas: The Origins and Evolution of Gazprom's Export Strategy' in Robert Mabro and Ian Wybrew-Bond (eds), *Gas to Europe: The Strategies of Four Major Suppliers* (Oxford: Oxford University Press, 1999), p. 190.
[3] Data for mid-1998, *Interfax Petroleum Report*, 5–11 June 1998, as quoted by Stern, 'Soviet and Russian Gas', p. 190.
[4] V. Kryukov and A. Moe, *Gazprom: Internal Structure, Management Principles and Financial Flows* (London: Royal Institute of International Affairs, 1996), pp. 71–2.

directly to consumers. This development is important with regard to greenhouse gas emissions as it also increases Gazprom's role in total Russian emissions. This is not necessarily a problem for Gazprom – quite the contrary. As argued in Chapter 5, it leaves the company in control over numerous sources of low-cost abatement projects.

An overwhelming problem in the domestic market is the non-payment situation. In 1998 only 28.5 per cent of delivered gas was paid for.[5] Less than half of this was paid for in cash.[6] Various alternative forms of payment are being developed: barter, transfer of shares and promissory notes. Gazprom is withholding taxes partly as a response to unpaid bills from state enterprises and organizations. The extremely complicated payment situation and all the various payment systems have made it exceedingly difficult to analyse, let alone penetrate, the Russian market. A forceful argument has been made that by its willingness to continue supplies on such terms, which in reality means a very low price for natural gas, Gazprom is subsidizing the entire Russian economy.[7]

Gazprom's greenhouse gas emissions

Gazprom can be affected by climate policies both because it will influence the markets for its products and because the emissions from its operations are large by any

[5] Gazprom, *Godovoy otschet.*
[6] Christiaan Vrolijk with Tobias Koch, *Russian Energy Prospects and the Implications for Emissions and Climate Policy*, Workshop Report (London: Royal Institute of International Affairs, 1999), p. 3.
[7] Clifford Gaddy and Barry W. Ickes, 'An Accounting Model of Russia's Virtual Economy', *Post-Soviet Geography and Economics*, March 1999, pp. 79–97.

standard. Data on the methane leakage from the vast Russian gas pipeline system are sparse and confusing. Until a few years ago data on leakage from the pipelines were not separated from the gas industry's own consumption of gas. This consumption occurs mainly at gas-fired compressor stations. A common rule of thumb has been that the industry consumes about 10 per cent of total throughput this way, i.e. some 60 BCM per year. But such numbers are only estimates because measuring at this point in the gas chain has not been a priority. Recently it was reported that 7.5 per cent of transported gas, some 44 BCM, is consumed by the compressor stations, and another 0.9 per cent, some 5.3 BCM, was reported as losses during transportation.[8]

According to the documentation for a project by the European Bank for Reconstruction and Development (EBRD) on upgrading the Russian unified gas supply system (the trunk pipeline network), Gazprom estimated its total methane losses in 1995 to be 1.4 per cent of production, some 7.8 BCM.[9] This figure is very similar to the data presented in a Gazprom analysis in 1997 giving leakage during transportation as 7.9 BCM in 1995, corresponding to 1.41 per cent of produced volume

[8] V. V. Remizov, 'Ekonomiya resursov prirodnogo gaza: energoeffektivnye tekhnologii', *Gazovaya Promyshlennost*, May 1999, p. 23.
[9] 'Unified Gas Supply System Upgrading, Russia', EBRD Project summary documents (downloaded 7 December 1999) from *http://www.ebrd.com/english/opera/psd/psd1996/57gazpro.htm*. The production figure refers to volumes of gas produced by Gazprom – 559. 5 BCM in 1995, or 94 per cent of the Russian total. The project was never started, and was officially cancelled in 1998, according to a communication from the EBRD in December 1999.

or 1.49 per cent of transported volume.[10] Gazprom's environmental report for 1998, based on analyses undertaken by it and Ruhrgas, estimated losses for the year to be less than 1.5 per cent of transported gas,[11] some 8.4 BCM. It set methane emissions in 1998 at 2.455 million tons.[12] It also estimated that the loss of methane during the production phase corresponded to 0.06 per cent of production volume, some 0.3 BCM.[13]

However, these data do not cover the entire Russian gas sector. According to the International Energy Agency's (IEA) survey of the Russian energy sector from 1995,[14] information from Rosgazifikatsiya (the umbrella organization for the regional and local distribution networks) suggested an annual loss of 3.5 BCM, with 80 per cent occurring on the premises of the customer and 20 per cent from the low-pressure network.[15] The IEA questions these figures, stating that they are probably too low. The data here are very uncertain, owing to lack of measuring systems.

In Table 6.1 we have attempted to estimate the GHG emissions from Gazprom's operations. As the table illustrates, the bulk of Gazprom's emissions consists of

[10] Yu. V. Kobzev, G.S. Akopova and N.G. Gadkaya (1997), 'Otsenka vybrosov metana v atmosferu obyektami RAO "Gazprom" v 1996 g.', *Gazovaya Promyshlennost*, no. 10, p. 70.
[11] Gazprom, 'Mezhdunarodnoye sotrudnichestvo v oblasti okhrany prirody', *Ekologicheskiy otschet 1998*. Downloaded from http://www.gazprom.ru/rus/ecology/1998.
[12] Ibid., 'Prirodookhrannaya deyatelnost 1998'.
[13] Ibid.
[14] 'Energy policies of the Russian Federation' (Paris: OECD/IEA, 1995), p. 171.
[15] Ibid.

Table 6.1: Greenhouse gas emissions from gas industry operations, 1998

	Methane (BCM)	Global warming potential (Mt CO_2 equivalent)
Leakages from production, high pressure trunk pipelines and compressor stations[a]	8	114
Fuel use at compressor stations on high-pressure trunk pipelines[b]	42	87
Total Gazprom emissions	50	201
Leakages during distribution[c]	5	66
Total gas industry emissions	43	267

[a] Gazprom, 'Mezhdunarodnoye sotrudnichestvo v oblasti okhrany prirody', *Ekologicheskiy otschet 1998*.
[b] V. V. Remizov, 'Ekonomiya resursov prirodnogo gaza: energoeffektivnye tekhnologii', *Gazovaya Promyshlennost*, May 1999, p. 23.
[c] See 'Energy policies of the Russian Federation', p. 171. In this report we have assumed that leakage during distribution, including leaks on the premises of the customer, is one-third larger than the numbers attributed to Rosgazifikatsia in the IEA report.

leakages of methane. Compared to CO_2, methane has a considerably higher global warming potential. When it is used for fuelling compressor stations, it is converted to CO_2 in the combustion process. Thus the methane that leaks out and is not combusted has a much greater impact on the global climate – the potential calculated in the second column – than the methane that is combusted. Of course there is much uncertainty with regard to the numbers in the table, particularly for

Table 6.2: Direct greenhouse gas emissions: Gazprom compared to other emitters

	Emissions (Mt CO_2 equivalents)		
	CO_2	Methane	Total
Russia[a]	1660	412	2152
Gazprom[b]	87	114	201
Shell[c]	97	11	109
Norway[d]	42	10	52

[a] Data for 1994, from *Vtoroye natsionalnoye soobschenie*.
[b] See Table 6.1.
[c] 1998 data from *http://www.shell.com/hse98/content/1,2174,1789-3883,00.html*.
[d] 1998 data, *http://www.ssb.no*.

leakage from low-pressure pipelines, for which data are sparse and unreliable. Nevertheless, the figures provide a general indication of the size of the emissions and their greenhouse effect.

Gazprom is directly responsible only for leaks and fuel use at the production sites and the high-pressure trunk pipelines, but these emissions are still sizeable. To put Gazprom's greenhouse gas emissions into perspective we have compared the company's direct emissions with those of several other emitters in Table 6.2. Emissions occurring during distribution and com-bustion are not included in the figures. As the table illustrates, Gazprom's direct emissions make up about 11 per cent of total Russian emissions measured in CO_2-equivalents. In sum, Gazprom's emissions are almost twice those of Shell and four times those of Norway.

In addition to the gas industry's own emissions there are the CO_2 emissions from the final consumer's combustion of natural gas. These were estimated to amount to approximately 575 $MtCO_2$ in 1998.

In view of the extent of its emissions it is not surprising that Gazprom has taken an interest in the climate issue. Over some years the industry's press has carried articles about the possibilities of reducing GHG emissions. This concern parallels what large companies in the West have done, partly as 'concerned corporate citizens' but also from fear that the climate regime will somehow create problems for them. The enormous role of gas in total emissions is probably also why Gazprom has been well represented in the Russian delegations to the climate negotiations.[16]

Is the industry structure sustainable?

Even though a technical potential for usage of the flexibility mechanisms by the Russian gas industry can be identified and an interest therein inferred, it must be asked if the industry is likely to have an organization that can facilitate this usage.

The Russian gas industry has gone through organizational changes and avoided others that make it stand out among the Russian energy industries. In 1992–3 Gazprom was transformed into what can be termed 'an autonomous state company'. It continued to perform the responsibilities of the gas ministry but it also took

[16] See *Directory of Participants of the Convention Bodies in the period July 1996 to December 1997*, Bonn, UNFCCC and FCCC/CP/1998/MISC.10.

over functions that had previously been the responsibility of the state, such as financing, development plans and exports. It seems that a general goal for the company was to secure maximum autonomy for itself.[17]

Another important aspect of Gazprom's development since 1992-3 has been the reinforcement of its monopoly position. The company has grown in many directions. It has taken over suppliers and has been especially active in converting previously military-oriented plants into suppliers of equipment for the oil and gas industry. The company has been involved in the establishment of several banks and has extensive interests in the Russian media. It is contemplating engagements in the electricity sector. This strategy gives Gazprom a special position in the Russian political system that adds to its importance as an energy supplier and an earner of export income, but it can also be argued that the company has overstretched its resources.

Even with an increased focus on the efficiency of current operations Gazprom will have to support new investment projects in order to be able to maintain present production levels and to increase them moderately in the longer term.[18] Of current production 85 per cent comes from fields with a declining output. Generally, the fields are becoming smaller and more complex. As a result of a tighter economy Gazprom has reconsidered

[17] For an elaboration, see Kryukov, and Moe, *Gazprom: Internal Structure.*
[18] The following paragraphs are based on Valery Kryukov and Arild Moe, 'Safeguarding Europe's supplies' in *Energy in the CIS and Eastern Europe – Yearbook 2000,* London: Petroleum Economist, June 2000, pp. 46-7.

its attitude to credits. In its first years of operation as a joint stock company the management board was almost entirely concerned with the accumulation of internal funds. An emphasis on acquiring foreign capital took place as of 1996, when the company approached the foreign capital markets. In the course of 1997 alone, credits for about $7 billion were raised through Credit Lyonnais, Dresdner Bank, Mannesmann and others. In 1996 it offered shares for sale through American depository receipts to institutional investors. After several attempts it has also succeeded in attracting investments from industrial partners. Ruhrgas bought 2.5 per cent of the shares in the company in 1998 and a further 1.5 per cent in 1999.[19] Altogether the German company has invested DM1160 million,[20] making it the single largest foreign investor in the Russian energy sector. In 1998, the maximum permitted combined share of foreign investors was raised from 9 to 14 per cent,[21] and in 1999 this share was raised to 20 per cent by the new law on gas supplies.[22] Towards the end of 1999 the share in Gazprom actually held by foreigners was about 6 per cent. The increasing role of Ruhrgas was further underlined when the German company's deputy chief executive, Burckhard Bergmann, became a member of Gazprom's board of directors in June 2000.[23]

[19] Ruhrgas AG Press Release, 25 May 1999.
[20] 660 million for the 2.5 per cent in 1998, *European Gas Markets*, 26 February 1999, p. 8; and DM500 million for the additional 1.5 per cent in 1999, *FT International Gas Report*, 28 May 1999, p. 7.
[21] Presidential decree No. 887 (1998), 'On the realization of shares in the open joint-stock company Gazprom'.
[22] Zakon 'O gazoznabzhenii', March 1999.
[23] Interfax Russian News, 30 June 2000.

The problems Gazprom faces with regard to investments are not only about finding interested investors but also about the fundamental premises for the operation of the company. Non-interference in exchange for stable performance has been the basis for Gazprom's existence as an all-encompassing *de facto* monopoly with export rights in the Russian gas industry. Gazprom has continued to supply gas to the domestic market at a low price or often for no payment at all, and it has continued to be a main source of revenue for the government. When this system was developed, the investment requirements in the industry seemed to be under control. But this impression was based on a false cost picture and on the fact that Gazprom could live on the huge investments made by the Soviet state without worrying about capital costs. Its position has become more and more difficult as fields are being depleted and pipelines are ageing. The company has been able to renew neither its resource base nor its infrastructure.

The various roles the company is (implicitly) supposed to play have become increasingly contradictory. At the same time as it is expected to supply gas at a low price or at no price at all, it is also supposed to be a basic source of revenue for the state. Taxes have had to be paid, not according to payment received but to the nominal price for the delivered gas. To fulfil its tax obligations Gazprom has even had to take up foreign credits. In addition it was awarded the role of tax collector for the state when an excise tax on gas was introduced in 1995. This situation has undermined the company's financial situation and its ability to invest. Paradoxically this has happened while its role in the country's economy, both as energy supplier and provider of revenue, has increased.

What Gazprom needs is a more flexible structure that will allow for sufficient realignment of maintenance and development while generating income. A radical transformation of domestic gas consumption is also necessary. This too will require much investment, as well as new 'rules of the game', but the yield in terms of conserved gas will be enormous.

Plausible scenarios for change in the Russian gas industry include separating transmission from production and sales. A larger role for independent or semi-independent companies in production and sales is also conceivable. But even a Gazprom that was reduced to operating the giant gas fields and developing major new fields would be the largest gas company in the world in terms of volume.

Even a break-up scenario for Gazprom does not necessarily change the implications for Russia's climate policy. In the context of this report one should be careful to distinguish between Gazprom and the Russian gas industry. Our argument is that even in the event of a major restructuring of the *company* Gazprom, the role of the *industry* will continue to be very big, and the argument for permitting the gas industry to take a share of the benefits from implementation of the Kyoto Protocol will be strong.

Export strategy

Because of weaknesses in the domestic market, exports play a disproportionately large role in Gazprom's operations and revenue. What implications for its possible participation in emissions trading or JI can be drawn from its export strategy and operations in foreign markets?

Gazprom is the dominant external supplier to the European gas market. It supplies some 46 per cent of imported gas to Germany, 40 per cent to Italy and 38 per cent to France. In central Europe it supplies almost 100 per cent of imported gas.

Soviet gas exports to the West expanded rapidly from the late 1970s and were based exclusively on long-term contracts. They were handled by a special foreign trade organization separate from the gas ministry. The goal of this organization was to maximize foreign revenue for the USSR.[24] At the same time as large gas export contracts were negotiated, other large-scale import deals for pipe and equipment to the Soviet gas industry were concluded. The gas and equipment contracts were not formally linked but were coordinated informally at a high political level. The notion of counter-trade, which is considered illegitimate and sometimes illegal in trade between Western countries, never had negative connotation in relations with the USSR: it resembled some of the trade mechanisms within the Soviet system. Thus in the history of Soviet and Russian gas exports, linkages between gas exports and imports are well known.

After the breakdown of the Soviet system and the abolition of the state's foreign trade monopoly, the gas

---

[24] On the organization and strategy of Soviet gas exports, see Javier Estrada, Helge Ole Bergesen, Arild Moe and Anne Kristin Sydnes, *Natural Gas in Europe: Markets, Organization and Politics* (London: Pinter Publishers, 1988), pp. 182–5.

trade organization was transferred to Gazprom under the name Gazeksport. The old contracts were honoured but it soon became clear that Gazprom now had somewhat different goals. It placed emphasis on downstream participation and created new alliances that were in conflict with established customers. This was most notable in Germany, where an alliance with Wintershall was formed and a joint company, Wingas, was established.[25] Various joint ventures were also formed in other countries; they gave Gazprom a presence in downstream operations and an insight into them that would have been unheard of in Soviet times.

Eastern Europe was treated quite separately from the West in Soviet foreign trade. Trade was negotiated as a large-scale barter arrangement within the framework of the trade agreements between the Soviet Union and the respective CMEA (Council for Mutual Economic Assistance) countries. With the dissolution of CMEA, Russia insisted that trade was converted to a regular money basis. This turned out to be very difficult for most of the countries in the former Eastern bloc. Gazprom's response was to create various joint companies and trading houses in these countries that could handle complex trade arrangements. These arrangements meant a return to bartering, but no longer within a national framework. The trading houses picked products that were needed by Gazprom directly or that Gazprom could easily sell inside Russia. And, unlike the practice in the Soviet period, gas was now priced according to the price level in Western markets and imported goods were

[25] Estrada et al, *The Development of European Gas Markets* (see ch. 3, n. 6 above), pp. 261–4.

priced 'realistically'. At the same time Gazprom acquired part-ownership in importing and distribution companies in these countries. The division between exporter and importer became blurred.[26]

These developments meant that Gazprom has changed from being an external supplier to the European markets to being an active participant in the importing countries. This strategy was very different from the Norwegian attitude, for example. The development of new companies and trading partners has been paralleled by a change in the delivery terms for gas. Russian gas sellers have become more flexible, offering gas on shorter-term contracts. All in all, Gazprom has emerged as a very flexible gas seller with very good connections in foreign markets.

In addition, it has repaired its relationship with Ruhrgas. As mentioned earlier, the German company became a significant shareholder in Gazprom in 1998. This development was explicitly connected with an extension of existing export contracts to 2030. According to Ruhrgas, 'we are now a strategic partner of Gazprom, with ties that go far beyond mere gas supply relations.'[27] The partnership may include upstream engagement with Ruhrgas in Russia. Gazprom has also formed alliances with Shell, Eni and Fortum. These are important developments too but not as comprehensive as the alliance with Ruhrgas, and they do not provide the same level of access to the key European gas markets.

[26] Kristian Tangen and Arild Moe, 'Russisk gass: Adferd i gassmarkedet – Nye strategier?', FNI Report (Lysaker: Fridtjof Nansen Institute, 1996).
[27] 'Ruhrgas looks upstream', 26 February 1999, *European Gas Markets*.

Ready for implementation?

In this chapter we have explained the 'objective' reasons why Gazprom is well placed to play an important role in Russia's implementation of the Kyoto Protocol and also to utilize the flexibility mechanisms of the protocol in its own interest. These reasons, in sum, are as follows:

- Gazprom controls a very big share of total Russian greenhouse gas emissions and accompanying abatement options.
- It has shown awareness of the climate problem and its own emissions, and it seems to be well informed about the international negotiations.
- It has a strong, centralized organization used to dealing with complex technological and financial projects.
- It strongly needs capital.
- Gazprom is so important a supplier of energy to the country and revenue to the state that its requirements must be taken very seriously by the authorities.
- At the same time, it enjoys more and more freedom of action.
- It has long experience in foreign trade and is used to coupling exports with various forms of barter and counter-trade.
- It has strong links downstream which could be relevant for emissions trading and joint implementation.
- Even if significant changes in the organization of the Russian gas industry are likely, the importance of the considerations above is not expected to change fundamentally.

We find that Gazprom has a very strong basis for participation in the implementation process. No other Russian sub-national actor has a comparable position. However, Gazprom has said little publicly about concrete plans for its participation. In the next chapter we shall spell out four scenarios for Gazprom's potential role and strategy.

7 GAS EXPORTS, EMISSIONS TRADING AND JI – FOUR SCENARIOS

We concluded in Chapter 6 that Gazprom institutionally is well placed to take advantage of the implementation of the Kyoto mechanisms. The Russian government may also have good reason to hand responsibility for the sale of quotas to Gazprom. In addition, it is possible that the implementation of climate policies in European countries could speed up the switch from coal to gas and consequently increase the demand for natural gas, although future demand growth will of course be the main determinant of Gazprom's exports to these markets. However, an analysis of overall future gas demand in Western Europe is outside the scope of this study. The purpose of this chapter is to discuss, by way of considering four scenarios, how Gazprom could use the Kyoto mechanisms in the interest of its core business of gas exports, i.e. how the implementation of Russia's climate policy could influence Gazprom's sale of gas to Europe.

We shall assume that there is a market and a demand for quotas, i.e. that Gazprom's partners either have a demand for quotas in order to offset their own emissions or that they want to sell the quotas into an international quota market. The size and functioning of the quota market will reflect the strategies chosen by individual countries to meet their Kyoto obligations. For example, in some countries gas power plants may not have to offset their emissions, and the companies operating them will have an opportunity to sell the quotas into the international quota market. Thus, the quotas will also have a value for actors who are not facing quota obligations.

In the first scenario we assume that Gazprom will be able to gain financially from participation in joint implementation projects and also from the sale of quotas: Russia's climate policy will mean increased revenue for it. In the second scenario Gazprom embarks on a strategy in which JI projects are actively used to forge strategic alliances with major purchasers of Russian gas. In the third scenario Gazprom is in control of a substantial share of Russia's quotas and combines the sale of quotas with the sale of gas. In the fourth scenario emission cuts as an element of Russian climate policy put pressure on the domestic Russian gas market, leaving Gazprom with a supply surplus which could find an outlet in the European markets. Although the company controls a share of Russia's quotas, there is no net economic benefit from this, as new taxes are introduced.

Scenario 1: quota sales as a source of income

If Gazprom acquires control of a substantial share of the surplus quotas and effectively implements abatement projects, it is likely that the total income from the sale of quotas and certificates could be $4–5 billion. However, the sale of quotas and certificates probably will not gain momentum before 2003 at the earliest. For the period 2003–2014, the annual income from quota sales for

Gazprom could be somewhere around $300–500 million. This compares to a yearly income of about $8 billion from gas exports to Europe. Clearly the flexibility mechanisms in the Kyoto Protocol could mean a substantial new source of income for the company.

In this scenario we assume that Gazprom obtains quotas and certificates worth $4 billion with 'no strings attached', i.e. the quotas and certificates can be and are actually sold directly into the international quota market that will develop. If, as we also assume, the income will be used for investments, how will the money be spent? As pointed out in Chapter 6, Gazprom's strategies in the past have to a large extent been volume-driven, not necessarily financially driven. This appears to be changing, but large extra revenues from the sale of quotas could mean that increased attention will be given to expanding the company's operations. There are many alternative uses to which Gazprom could apply this extra income including developing new production capacity, upgrading pipelines and downstream acquisitions. However, as described in Chapter 6, the company's financial position has been constrained for several years. This has led Gazprom, reluctantly, into the international credit market. In this perspective an extra infusion of capital would most probably replace new credits, thus having no direct implication for exports.

Scenario 2: joint implementation and industrial cooperation

Compared with other major energy companies such as Shell and BP Amoco,[1] Gazprom has taken few initiatives to gain experience in the field of emissions trading and joint implementation. The most substantial move in this respect has been a project undertaken jointly by Gazprom and Ruhrgas.[2] The main purpose of this project has been to reduce the energy needed to transport natural gas by optimizing grid operations. Reduced gas consumption also leads to substantial cuts in greenhouse gas emissions, and in 1997 the project was recognized as a JI project under the pilot phase. In its first phase, it focused on a section of the Gazprom high-pressure gas pipeline system to the east of Moscow in the Nizhny Novgorod region. This system is operated by Volgotransgaz, a regional transmission organization within Gazprom.

Every year some 160 billion cubic metres of gas is transported through Volgotransgaz's Uzhgorod Corridor. Until now roughly 3 billion cubic metres of fuel gas has been consumed yearly by the compressor stations. Through grid optimization, fuel gas consumption was

[1] Both these companies have established internal systems for emissions trading and have participated in several projects with the aim of reducing greenhouse gas emissions.
[2] Yevgeniy Dedikov and Jan Kätelhön, 'Reducing the Burden on the Environment by Optimising Gas Transmission', paper presented at the IEA workshop on opportunities for international cooperation under the Kyoto Protocol, Moscow, 1–2 October 1998. The project is also presented in 'Gazprom and Ruhrgas Make an Important Contribution to Carbon Dioxide Reduction', Ruhrgas press release, 25 October 1999.

reduced by 131 million cubic metres a year, with a corresponding annual decrease in carbon dioxide emissions of 231,000 tonnes. The project has led to annual fuel savings worth some US$7 million if exported. If the appropriate legal conditions are established for joint implementation projects, Gazprom intends, together with Ruhrgas, to extend these measures to large parts of its pipeline system. According to estimates, about 3.6 million tonnes of CO_2 emissions could then be avoided annually.

The Ruhrgas-Gazprom pilot JI project gives Gazprom practical experience in carrying out such projects and also illustrates their potential. It is also an indication of improved relations between Ruhrgas and Gazprom after years when these have been strained, and the German side has emphasized this aspect of the project.[3] Although its scope, financially as well as environmentally, is limited, the project could have important implications for Gazprom's future role in Russian emissions trading. The second scenario takes this project as its point of departure.

As pointed out above, the potential for gains in efficiency within the Russian gas industry is extremely large. Gazprom may want to embark on a strategy in which this potential is used actively to forge ties with major companies downstream. These projects would contain

[3] 'On the whole, the project has been extremely gratifying. This may be due to the fact that both partners, Gazprom and Ruhrgas, have a strong desire to cooperate, which is why other projects have also been successful. This close co-operation creates an atmosphere of mutual trust and understanding which is indispensable for projects of this kind.' Dedikov and Kätelhön, 'Reducing the Burden'.

several interesting features for both parties. Gazprom would receive investments in efficiency measures and possibly also emission reduction units (ERUs) that it could sell in line with the reasoning in Scenario 1. At the same time the partners in such projects, those companies possessing the relevant technology, would likely be big transmission companies, i.e. important customers for Russian gas.

For the foreign partner, e.g. Ruhrgas, these projects would offer the potential of acquiring ERUs which can either be used to offset its own obligations with regard to emission cuts or be sold by the transmission company downstream, thus making it possible to offer CO_2-free gas to the consumer. Other factors remaining unchanged, participation in these projects would make Russian gas more attractive for this kind of buyer. The link to increases in export volumes would not have to be explicit, but linking the amounts of gas saved from a project to increased deliveries would seem a natural possibility.[4] These JI projects would thus increase industrial cooperation in a way that directly or indirectly could be of competitive advantage to Russian gas in selected export markets.

Scenario 3: quota sales and gas exports

In this scenario we assume that Gazprom acquires control over a large share of the surplus quotas. As indicated in

[4] Linking volume gains from efficiency investments in the pipeline system to export deliveries was in fact explored in a deal between Gazprom and Italian ENI in 1994, according to Estrada et al., *The Development of European Gas Markets*, p. 270.

Chapter 5, the distribution of these quotas to various entities in the Russian economy is a possible scenario, especially if the central authorities remain weak. But Gazprom does not use these quotas solely as a welcome source of revenue. The quotas are not sold on the international quota market. Instead, they are used for expanding the company's position in the gas market.

Projects along the lines of the Ruhrgas–Gazprom JI project could also be the point of departure for the evolution of such schemes. Within the framework of large-scale industrial cooperation, Gazprom's quotas could be used for a variety of purposes. Quota transfers could be linked to foreign investments in Russian upstream capacity and also to new export contracts. Another opportunity would be for Gazprom to link the sale of gas and quotas directly in the same contract. Gazprom is actually in a position in which it can offer the market 'CO_2-free' natural gas, i.e. the CO_2 emissions from natural gas combustion are offset by quotas.[5] Unlike the second scenario, in which a foreign partner handles the quotas, Gazprom takes direct advantage of this possibility itself. In short, climate change cooperation between the world's largest gas producer and exporter (which is also a large GHG emitter) and major customers appears to open up a range of opportunities beneficial to both parties.

Judging from statements by its representatives, Ruhrgas seems well aware of these opportunities. It appears

---

[5] British gas suppliers have offered CO_2-free gas, basically for its marketing effect. Within a future CO_2-restricted energy sector, however, there could be a larger market for this service.

eager to expand the existing cooperation on climate change as well as in other areas. Of course, its main motivation for fostering cooperation is not just the opportunities arising from quota trading and JI; a strong alliance between Ruhrgas and Gazprom could be a major driving force in the European energy market. But climate change could become an important component of such an alliance.

With regard to the sale of surplus quotas, why would Gazprom pursue such a complicated strategy? Why not sell the quotas and use the revenues as depicted in the first scenario? Gazprom's financial operations have been followed closely by the Russian government. If surplus quotas were given to Gazprom 'with no strings attached', this could mean the introduction of new taxes and regulations. From this perspective, it would be beneficial for the company to keep its sources of income opaque. Quotas sold directly on the international quota market would create a cash flow easy to trace and tax. It would be harder to determine the value created by quota transfers taking place within the framework of joint industrial projects in which quotas are given in exchange for investments, hardware, market shares, etc. Thus, one motivation for disguising quota sales could be the same as why much of Russian energy is paid through barter agreements – to avoid taxation.

A strategy in which surplus quotas are used to expand the market for Russian gas would also be a strong argument for obtaining the quotas from the government in the first place. By pursuing this line of argument, Gazprom can claim that surplus quotas can be used to generate wealth that benefits Russian society and also creates revenue for the state. Consequently it should be left in control of at least a share of the surplus quotas.

Quotas do not, however, have to be derived from surplus quotas. It is equally possible that Gazprom can produce significant emission reductions entirely on its own by low-cost measures. But before an international quota market is established it will have no interest in doing this. When a market is established Gazprom will have a strong argument that it should be left in control of permits derived from its own reductions. As long as the Russian economy remains in the 'transition stage', the real cost of achieving emission reductions may be disguised. Gazprom will have every reason to exaggerate the cost. Once it controls the quotas, they may be used in the same way as described above for 'hot air' quotas.

Scenario 4: climate change as a threat to Gazprom's operations

According to the analysis in previous chapters of this report, Gazprom appears well positioned to gain from the implementation of a Russian climate policy. This is the case in the first three scenarios. However, other scenarios can be depicted too.

Owing to the large emissions from Gazprom's own operations and from the emissions arising from domestic Russian gas combustion, the company is in principle vulnerable if a comprehensive and strong Russian climate policy is implemented. If climate taxes are introduced instead of quota systems, the climate issue could become an economic burden for it, drawing on its strained equity and also eroding the domestic Russian market. However, we do not consider effective implementation of a strict Russian climate policy to be very likely.

What is conceivable is that Gazprom obtains control over a portion of the Russian quotas but at the same time remains subject to CO_2 taxation, meaning that it acquires no net economic benefit from quota sales. CO_2 taxation on general consumption seems a more remote possibility so long as neither the price nor the payment system functions. However, CO_2 taxation, whether applied only within the gas industry or more broadly, would result in reduced domestic gas consumption.

In such a situation Gazprom would face a supply surplus in the domestic market but would have limited means for financing an expansion of consumption. This could put pressure on exports and thereby reduced gas prices and increased competition in the market. With the completion of the new pipeline through Belarus and Poland and of other planned pipeline projects, transport capacity will be less of a constraint than it has been for many years.

This line of reasoning is akin to the theory of the Russian 'gas bubble' – the oversupply of Russian gas[6] – according to which a strong supply push to the export markets should have taken place long ago. This has not happened. And even in a scenario with a strict Russian climate policy one must be careful not to exaggerate the direct impact on exports. An adjustment in output is

[6] See Estrada, *The Development of European Gas Markets*, pp. 270-1.

another possible response to oversupply. The point here is that under such a scenario the push to sell more in the export market will be stronger than would have been the case in the absence of strict domestic climate measures.

8 CONCLUSIONS

Currently Russia's climate policy contains few long-term strategies. In international negotiations the Russian position has shifted and been inconsistent. It appears to have been dominated largely by the views of a few agencies – and even individual negotiators. At the domestic level numerous climate programmes have been initiated and approved. However, the lack of a clear implementation strategy and sufficient funding brings us to believe that these programmes have had little impact in terms of real emission reductions.

We find it likely that Russia will have a considerable volume of quotas for sale in a future international market, even without implementing domestic climate change measures. However, the official Russian position, as well as a widespread perception among Russian experts, appears to be that future economic growth will require increased energy consumption and that there will be little or no 'hot air' when the first commitment period starts, i.e. Russia's 'business-as-usual' emissions in 2008–12 will be at the 1990 level. The authors of this report question this position and find it likely that future emissions levels will be considerably lower.

If emissions remain below the 1990 level, the Kyoto Protocol can, somewhat coincidentally, mean substantial additional revenue for Russia. Not only will it have a large volume of emission quotas for sale, but also it will likely be the dominant seller of quotas, enabling it to take a monopoly rent.

How surplus quotas should be handled is controversial within Russia. Many Russian actors see the sale of surplus quotas as a threat to future economic growth. In line with this view, the surplus quotas (if there are any) should be saved to offset emission growth in future commitment periods. Furthermore, some see the sale of surplus quotas as a threat to joint implementation projects. These projects are expected to yield badly needed investments in efficiency and modernization. Compared to emissions trading, which seems abstract and 'unreal' to many actors, joint implementation appears easier to understand, as it represents concrete projects with investments in energy efficiency measures and real emissions reductions. Thus in Russia, as in the international arena, strong forces favour joint implementation over the unrestricted sale of quotas. These underlying conflicts are likely to heat up as implementation of the Kyoto Protocol draws closer.

How the sale of quotas will be carried out, and what the framework for joint implementation projects will look like is uncertain yet. The 'implementation battle' has just commenced, and most domestic actors have not yet taken a decisive position on how they would like the protocol to be implemented. For most of them, the climate regime represents issues that are vague and hard to grasp. There is little knowledge of the Kyoto Protocol, its possible implications and opportunities. However, we argue that for several reasons the energy industries are in a good position to gain from the future implementation of a Russian climate policy. Among the energy companies Gazprom is in an especially favourable position. The company has practical experience, institutional capacity and also good arguments for being left in control of a large share of Russia's quotas.

In this respect, Gazprom has two very important resources, namely the present emissions of the gas industry and influence on emissions from gas consumption. Abatement measures can be converted into quotas that may have a price far above the costs of achieving emission cuts, or they may be used to form strategic industrial partnerships.

Exactly how Gazprom will use these quotas and how this will affect Russian gas export strategies are subjects of speculation. For this purpose we developed four scenarios, but did not attempt to quantify the consequences for export trade and gas prices. Three of the four scenarios indicate that in implementing the Kyoto mechanisms, Russia is likely to put more of its gas on the market. In two scenarios the competitive position of Russian gas in relation to other suppliers is improved following the application of these mechanisms. In one scenario Gazprom is more or less forced to sell more gas abroad, with negative effects on the market price.

Elaborating in detail how and to what extent Gazprom's control over quotas will influence the European gas market is outside the scope of this report. But the general findings of this study are important: Gazprom is in a good position to achieve control over a valuable new 'commodity', i.e. cheap or cost-free emission quotas. This can result in a range of new opportunities for it.

Although this report has put special emphasis on Gazprom's potential, other Russian companies, especially in the energy sector, could also reap considerable benefits from climate politics. The distribution of revenue that could come from the Kyoto mechanisms is likely to be an important issue in Russian politics in the years ahead.

JAPAN AND THE KYOTO PROTOCOL
Conditions for Ratification

Hiroshi Matsumura

Many industrialized countries will start the process of ratifying the Kyoto Protocol on the basis of the outcome of the negotiations at the Sixth Conference of Parties in The Hague, in November 2000. Policy-makers in most of these countries will face domestic hurdles including the trade-off between political commitments and economic realities. The Japanese government (host to the Kyoto negotiations) is facing a serious problem in meeting its targets, because of the Tokaimura nuclear disaster and resulting unwillingness to expand nuclear capacity. This report analyses the specific conditions for Japan, covering various scenarios for additional policies such as fuel switching, carbon taxation and emissions trading, within the context of a liberalizing energy market. It also speculates on the future of the Kyoto regime itself.

Published October 2000　　　ISBN 1 86203 125 8
price £12.50

THE ROYAL INSTITUTE OF
INTERNATIONAL AFFAIRS
Energy and Environment Programme